RAND

The Economic Dimensions of National Security

C. R. Neu, Charles Wolf, Jr.

Prepared for the
Office of the Secretary of Defense

National Defense
Research Division

PREFACE

On February 7 and 8, 1992, a conference was convened at RAND in Santa Monica, California, to discuss "The Economic Dimensions of National Security." Participants in the conference came from the academic community, the federal government, the private sector, and research institutions. (A list of participants is provided in the Appendix.)

The end of the Cold War and the associated dramatic changes in the geopolitical environment have led many observers to conclude that much of our past thinking about U.S. national security interests and policies is now outmoded and that a fundamental rethinking of these interests and policies is required. In particular, the notion is becoming widespread that economic factors and concerns will play a more prominent role in defining and pursuing U.S. national security objectives. The authors' aim in convening the RAND conference was to advance understanding of the emerging "economic dimensions" of U.S. national security policymaking.

The aim of this report is the same. It is meant as a contribution to the task of defining a useful frame of reference for what will undoubtedly be a continuing discussion of the relation between economics and national security. Although it is not intended as a summary of conference proceedings, this report draws heavily on the ideas and hypotheses put forward during the conference. In accordance with the ground rules established at the conference, the authors have not attributed any of the ideas noted in this report to particular conference participants. They have tried to retain the exploratory and speculative tone of the conference discussions. They offer hypotheses as well as facts. Ultimately, this report and the conference that preceded it may prove more useful for the questions they generate than for the conclusions they reach.

Both the original conference and this report were supported by the Office of the Under Secretary of Defense for Policy. Both were parts of the International Economic Policy program of RAND's National Defense Research Institute, a federally funded research and development center sponsored by the Office of the Secretary of Defense, the Joint Staff, and the defense agencies.

CONTENTS

TABLES

iv

The end of the Cold War has brought a reduction in the direct military and political threats facing the United States. As these threats have receded, the attention of both the U.S. policy community and the general public has turned to other kinds of developments and circumstances that can affect the ability of the U.S. population to pursue life, liberty, happiness, and prosperity on their own terms. In particular, recent years have seen increased interest in U.S. "economic security"—in the ability of the United States to protect its own economic prosperity and to shape the international economic environment to the advantage of most of the U.S. population. Increasing attention is being paid to defining U.S. economic interests and to identifying potential threats to these interests. Increasing attention is also being paid to the usefulness of economic instruments as substitutes for or complements to military and political means of achieving traditional U.S. national-security and foreign-policy objectives. Increasingly, the first responses to national-security and foreign-policy problems are economic: trade restrictions, embargoes, freezing of financial assets, and so on. This new emphasis on economic means for achieving international ends raises new questions about what constitutes national "economic power" and how such power can and should be exercised.

WHAT IS ECONOMIC SECURITY?

Economic security is the ability to protect or to advance U.S. economic interests in the face of events, developments, or actions that may threaten or block these interests. These challenges or obstacles may be foreign or domestic in origin, intentional or accidental, and the consequences of human or of natural forces. Further, economic security depends on the United States' ability to shape the international economic environment to its liking—for example, by playing a major role in establishing the rules that govern international economic relations and by using economic means to influence the policies (economic and otherwise) of other countries. Economic security also requires possessing the material resources to fend off noneconomic challenges. Among other things, one must have the economic wherewithal to support an adequate military.

Certainly, economic prosperity as usually defined—economic growth, full employment, low inflation, high levels of investment, improvements in productivity, etc.—will contribute to economic security. But economic security requires more than just maximizing current economic prosperity. The objective of economic security is to reduce uncertainty about continued economic well-being. Sometimes it will be wise to sacrifice some current prosperity to make that of the future more stable, more certain, or less subject to loss.

PURSUING ECONOMIC SECURITY

Much discussion of economic security is couched in terms of international competition and comparisons: Which economies are biggest, most productive, most innovative? Who controls important economic assets? What firms are dominant in particular markets? This focus on competition and comparisons is useful in identifying at least some policies that will enhance U.S. economic security.

The Importance of Relative Size

Few would contend that U.S interests would have been better served if the U.S. economy stood today in the same relation to other economies as it did in, say, 1950—if, that is, the postwar reconstruction of Europe and Asia or economic development efforts elsewhere had been less successful. The United States also has an interest in promoting economic reform and growth in the formerly socialist countries. Nonetheless, neither U.S. nor world interests will be served if U.S. economic growth lags behind that of the rest of the industrialized world.

Nations with large economies naturally enjoy greater influence in establishing the rules that govern international economic relations. Dominant in nearly every dimension of economic activity in the early postwar era, the United States played a key role in establishing the international economic institutions and arrangements that still shape international economic activity. By and large, the United States has been a benevolent and effective maker of international economic rules, and one might well wonder who will fill this role if the United States no longer does. To some observers, it is no coincidence that international cooperation in economic matters has become more problematic in the latter part of the postwar era as U.S. economic dominance has become less pronounced.

In recent years, investment as a share of total output has been lower in the United States than in most other industrialized countries. If this pattern persists, economic growth in the United States will almost certainly lag behind growth elsewhere in the world. The relative size of the U.S. economy—and with it U.S. influence in international economic matters—will decrease. The effective pursuit of U.S. economic security, and probably of broader, international economic security as well, will require U.S. economic policies that restrain consumption, encourage saving, and provide incentives for investment.

Support for Specific Industries

Beyond measures to raise the general level of investment in the United States, interest is growing in direct government support for specific "strategic" or "critical" industries. Allegedly, such support will enhance U.S. economic security by promoting the growth of industries that will particularly contribute to U.S. economic welfare— by generating high-paying jobs, higher-than-usual profits, or "spinoffs" beneficial to other industries. Further, such support may prove an effective counter to efforts by foreign governments to boost their own domestic activity in the same industries.

As a theoretical principle, the possibility that direct government support of particular industries can enhance overall national welfare is well established. But support for one industry must necessarily come at the expense of other industries or interests (subsidies paid to a favored industry, for example, must be financed by someone), and there is considerable debate today over whether the potential benefits of such support are sufficient to outweigh the inevitable costs. There is also considerable suspicion over governments' ability to identify opportunities for welfare-enhancing industrial support objectively and to provide that support effectively. We can have little confidence that increased governmental efforts to support particular industries will prove beneficial.

Without question, other nations aggressively support particular industries, and U.S. firms and U.S. workers suffer as a consequence. This fact alone, though, is not sufficient to justify similar support by the U.S. government. In some cases, foreign industrial policies may benefit U.S. consumers, and a careful (and inevitably political) balancing of consumers' gains against producers' losses will be required. Even when it seems clear that foreign actions are detrimental to U.S. interests, the best U.S. response is not necessarily to provide counterbalancing help to the U.S. industry most directly affected by foreign subsidies. In some cases, it may be better for the United States to retaliate in some other area, seeking not simply to balance or cancel out the effects of a foreign subsidy but rather to bring about the removal of the foreign subsidy that caused the problem in the first place. As in military affairs, capitalizing on one's own strengths or exploiting an opponent's weaknesses may prove a more effective counter than trying to meet an opponent's challenge head-on.

Maintaining an Adequate Military

Military strength requires an economic underpinning, and a part of economic security is maintaining a level of general economic output that allows diversion of adequate resources to military uses.

At a more micro level, economic security will also require maintenance of the industrial capability to design and to produce successive generations of technologically sophisticated weapons. It is only in the last few years, as defense spending has been sharply reduced, that serious attention has been turned to understanding what industrial capabilities are truly essential to this task and what will be required to maintain these capabilities. Efforts to date to identify particular technologies as "critical" for defense purposes have not yielded much in the way of operational policies for managing the defense industrial base. General policies aimed at narrowing the gap between military and commercial technology development efforts and at attracting additional firms into supplying military needs are likely to be more productive than efforts to preserve particular firms or to advance particular technologies.

As defense spending declines further, it will probably also be wise to make greater use of foreign suppliers to meet U.S. military needs. For some military needs, of course, it will never be wise to rely on foreign sourcing. But for many purposes, developing sources of supply in friendly nations may reduce Department of Defense (DoD) dependency on domestic monopolists and create additional opportunities for expanded production if it should ever become necessary to rebuild U.S. military forces.

Foreign Investment in the United States

For the most part, fears about foreign direct investment in the United States appear to be unfounded. Although foreign interests may gain control of significant commercial or industrial assets in the United States through direct investment, it is far from obvious who gains effective leverage over whom as a result of such transactions. Fixed assets in the United States cannot be easily withdrawn by a foreign owner, and a foreign owner of U.S. assets is in a very real sense hostage to U.S. laws and policies. Although research on the subject is far from complete, there seems little evidence to date that the behavior of foreign-owned firms operating in the United States differs from that of similar U.S.-owned firms—at least not in ways that can be viewed as contrary to U.S. interests. Rather than being dangerous, foreign investment can bring real benefits to the U.S. economy. To the extent that foreign investment results in the creation of new fixed assets in the United States or the introduction to this country of superior foreign methods or processes, employment opportunities for and the productivity of U.S. workers is likely to be increased.

A BROADER VIEW OF ECONOMIC SECURITY

True economic security will require more than just making sure that the U.S. economy is bigger, more robust, or faster growing than other economies; more than just assuring that U.S. firms are dominant in important world markets; more than maintaining military forces that are superior to those of any potential challengers. In addition to trying to keep the U.S. economy "Number 1" and doing what we can to limit our vulnerability to negative external developments, we should also seek ways to minimize international instability of the sort that will generate undesirable developments in the first place. U.S. economic security can be enhanced by enhancing international economic security. In particular, U.S. economic security should aim to achieve the following objectives.

Maintaining Access to Foreign Markets

The economic well-being of the U.S. population depends to a large degree on their access—as both buyers and sellers—to international goods and financial markets. The increasing integration of the U.S. economy into the larger global economy unquestionably creates susceptibilities to shocks emanating elsewhere in the world. But withdrawal or isolation from foreign markets would do more harm to U.S. interests than would any of these shocks. U.S. economic security policy should not aim, therefore, at trying to reduce U.S. "dependence" on foreign sources of supply. Rather, the objective should be to make continued access to foreign markets more certain. The U.S. should seek to strengthen international cooperation on trade matters, to make continuous and tangible progress toward expanding world trade, and to ensure that international trade is governed by understandable and predictable rules rather than by the changeable whims of national governments.

Creating a Stable International Financial Environment

Because financial markets have become truly global, stable and well-functioning U.S. financial markets are possible only within a stable and well-functioning international financial environment. Of particular concern in recent years have been exchange-rate volatility and the large and unpredictable international capital movements that cause exchange-rate fluctuations. There is no consensus regarding the most effective approaches to controlling these sorts of instability, but there is a growing recognition that exchange-rate stability, and international financial stability more generally, will be achieved only through increased cooperation among policymakers in the world's industrialized economies. Such cooperation will necessarily involve some loss of national freedom of action in economic matters. Ironically, though, giving up some national sovereignty in this regard will probably be essential to the pursuit of international financial stability and thus to the pursuit of national economic security.

Promoting Market-Oriented Economic Policies

For a variety of reasons, the United States has an interest in promoting market-oriented economic policies in other countries. Although private international capital markets have expanded greatly in the last twenty years, these private markets are still inadequate to meet the needs of countries trying, after years of state-dominated economic failure, to establish new, market-oriented approaches to economic activity. At least for the immediate future, U.S. economic security will require continued support of the official multilateral institutions—like the World Bank and the International Monetary Fund—that seek to fill gaps in private credit markets and to encourage market-oriented solutions to economic problems in developing and reforming economies. In addition, continuing efforts to reform these institutions and to improve their operations should be aggressively pursued. For some purposes, it may also be necessary to create new multilateral channels for financing development and reform efforts.

Maintaining a Functioning International Commercial and Financial Infrastructure

The economic well-being of the U.S. population depends on the smooth conduct of national and international commerce and finance, and hence on the smooth and efficient functioning of what one might think of as a commercial and financial infrastructure. U.S. policy continues to promote the traditional requirements of international commerce and finance, such as the freedom of peaceful international passage and the sanctity of property. Recent years have seen, however, growing policy interest in a broad range of international regulatory matters that are relevant to the conduct of international economic activity. In particular, attention has, appropriately,

focused on closing gaps in the regulation of international banking
activity, reducing the vulnerability of electronic clearing arrangements (the so-called financial wires) to intentional or accidental disruption, strengthening protection of intellectual property rights, establishing workable enforcement mechanisms for international trade
agreements, and devising a framework for effective international
competition (anti-trust) policy.

An Equitable Distribution of Domestic Income

True national security—of either the military or the economic variety—requires a unified populace with a common understanding of
national interests and capable of standing together in the face of
foreign challenges. This kind of unity will be promoted by a domestic distribution of income and economic well-being that is perceived
to be broadly fair. Although the continuing integration of the U.S.
economy into the broader international economy has unquestionably benefited most of the U.S. population, lower-skilled U.S. workers increasingly find themselves in competition with an enormous
pool of low-skilled and low-paid labor in the rest of the world. If
these workers are left out of the general prosperity, U.S. economic
security will be undermined. Efforts to raise the skill levels and
hence the productivity of such workers should be a principal aim of
U.S. economic security policies. Unfortunately, few efforts to raise
the productivity of adult workers have proven successful, and re-
vamping the U.S. educational system to produce a new generation of
highly productive workers—even if anyone knew how to effect such a
transformation—will produce results only years in the future. While
waiting for such efforts to bear fruit, we may wish to rethink the conventional wisdom that economic security is advanced by promoting
"high-tech" industries. A wiser strategy might be to work to increase
productivity, and thus wages, in industries that can provide jobs,
possibly of a distinctly "low-tech" variety, for those U.S. workers who
are most sorely pressed by low-wage foreign competition.

ECONOMIC POWER

Thus far, we have focused on one aspect of economic security: the
broad national-security consequences of economic policies. The
DoD is, organizationally, a secondary player in this arena. But

"economic security" also has another dimension: the economic consequences of national security policies. Defense policies are more directly involved here, and the DoD and the National Security Council are dominant players in this arena.

The economic consequences of national security policies have two components: first, the ways in which military instruments may be used to generate economic effects and second, ways in which economic instruments can be used to substitute for, or to complement, military instruments in pursuit of security objectives.

Using Defense Resources for Economic Purposes

The first component focuses on how economic considerations can affect the management, use and allocation of resources earmarked for defense purposes. For example, can military research and development programs be configured in ways that make them more likely to generate commercially valuable "spin-offs"? Can military resources—troops, airlift, logistics, engineering and medical services, for example—be more effectively used to support nontraditional objectives—emergency assistance, economic development, or nation-building perhaps—without significantly diminishing their combat effectiveness? Can U.S. arms production and export policies be structured so as to discourage production or acquisition of particularly dangerous weapons by other nations? Can extensive U.S. intelligence assets be effectively and appropriately used for economic purposes?

Using Economic Instruments for Defense Purposes

The second component involves the potential use of economic instruments as substitutes for, or complements of, military instruments. As elements of security policy, economic instruments can influence the behavior of other countries by conferring economic benefits or imposing economic costs, or by displaying a credible capacity to do so. Foreign economic as well as military aid, technical assistance, and most-favored nation status can be used to confer such benefits. And economic sanctions—embargoes, freezing of financial assets, restricting access to U.S. markets, or heavily taxing such access—can be used to impose economic costs. When economic instruments are used as adjuncts of security policy, they can be compared to military instruments. Military instruments also provide a means of influencing behavior in the international arena by deterrence or compellence: that is, by using force, or credibly threatening to use it, to dissuade other countries from using force, or by using force to coerce, preempt, or repel their attempts to use it.

There are opportunities, which are sometimes overlooked, for using economic instruments—whether as "carrots" or "sticks"—to enhance the effectiveness of military instruments in the pursuit of security objectives. However, government entities that control the levers of economic power are not always those that are used to thinking in military or foreign-policy terms. Careful coordination of economic and military instruments for the effective employment of both will require mechanisms for policy planning and interagency cooperation that are infrequently exercised today.

ACKNOWLEDGMENTS

The authors wish to express appreciation for the knowledgeable, valuable, and extensive comments on an earlier draft by RAND colleagues Michael Kennedy and Julia Lowell, as the formal reviewers of this report. Their suggestions, as well as the equally valuable ones provided informally to us by Harold Brown, have contributed measurably to improving the report's quality.

Chapter One

NATIONAL SECURITY, NATIONAL INTERESTS, AND ECONOMICS

The late 1980s and the early 1990s have brought important changes in how the U.S. population views the world and its interests. In particular, we have changed the way we think about national security—what it is, how to pursue it, and what threatens it.

Traditionally, we have thought about national security primarily in military and political terms. The principal threats to U.S. national security were posed by the military forces, the political ideologies, and the foreign policies of actual or potential adversaries.

All this is changing. The end of the Cold War and the breakup of the Soviet empire have eliminated or much reduced the primary political and military threats the United States faced in recent years. The Russian Federation, of course, retains a massive nuclear arsenal; however, for the time being at least, no use or threatened use of these weapons against the United States seems plausible. The struggle for world leadership that dominated the postwar period now appears to be over. Political and military challenges remain, of course, as the Persian Gulf crisis demonstrated, and military powers remain in the world that can mount serious threats to U.S. interests, if not to the United States itself. Nonetheless, it is hard to argue with the proposition that military and political threats to U.S. interests have significantly declined.

ECONOMIC SECURITY

If the principal military and political adversary has disappeared, what remains to threaten U.S. national interests? If the possibility of armed confrontation with the Soviet Union no longer limits U.S. freedom of action in the world, what does constrain us?

Certainly, military and political developments throughout the world remain of concern to the United States. Certainly, U.S. freedom of action continues to be limited in some places and circumstances by political or military opposition. But as military and political threats have declined, we have turned our attention increasingly to other kinds of developments. In particular, today when we think about external events, actions, or developments that could cause injury to members of the U.S. population or to their ability to pursue life, liberty, happiness, or prosperity on their own terms, we think about economic matters. Both policymakers and the broader public seem less concerned these days about surprise attack and more about the loss of U.S. jobs to a foreign country, less about foreign military bases and more about access to foreign markets, less about other countries' military alliances and more about their preferential trading arrangements, less about policies designed to create military advantage and more about policies designed to create commercial advantage. It is fashionable (if not entirely accurate) to say that the principal threats to U.S. national interests today are economic rather than political or military.

Similarly, some argue that, with the passing of the Soviet threat, the ability of the United States to pursue its national interests and to shape the world to its liking is limited principally by its own willingness to act and by its ability to bear the costs of action. These, in turn, may be strongly influenced by economic circumstances. If the economy falters, will the United States still be willing to bear the costs of maintaining the military forces necessary to preserve world order (or, more realistically, to counter the more egregious threats to this order)? If there are too many unmet material needs at home, will the United States spare resources to aid economic reform in Eastern Europe and the former Soviet Union? If some U.S. citizens are left out of the general prosperity, will the United States have the national unity to meet foreign challenges?

Efforts to protect or to promote U.S. economic interests in the international arena are, of course, not new. Since its foundation, this country has pursued policies to promote access to foreign markets, dependable supplies of essential commodities, freedom of commercial passage, advantageous trading relationships, international economic stability, and other economic interests. Likewise, its people have always recognized a connection between their economic circumstances and their ability to influence international events. During the last few years, however, there has been a noticeable refocusing of national attention—clearly evident during the recent presidential campaign—on the economic components and consequences of U.S. international relations. To use the currently fashionable phrase, the United States is now paying more attention to matters of economic security.

This has happened, in part, because we now have the luxury of adopting a somewhat more relaxed attitude with regard to military and foreign-policy interests. The United States is now free to place greater emphasis on the pursuit of its economic interests. Calls to use the "peace dividend" for domestic programs are only the most obvious manifestations of this emerging attitude.

Beyond this, recent events have provided some forceful reminders of the connection between a country's economic performance and its ability to pursue the traditional aims of national-security policy: maintaining and projecting military forces, influencing the behavior of other nations, controlling its own destiny, and generally remaining a great power. It was, after all, the economic failures of Communist regimes that were in large measure responsible for the decline in the military and political power of the Soviet Union and its former allies.

Interest in economic security has been further heightened by what many have seen as the disappointing performance of the U.S. economy in recent years—both in absolute terms and relative to other industrialized economies. Recognition is growing that other economies—Germany and Japan in particular—will face some daunting economic challenges in the next few years. Still, we have learned that a U.S. economy that is dependably more robust and more dynamic than economies elsewhere in the world cannot be taken for granted. We are also becoming more aware that the economic conditions in which we live are not entirely "made in the U.S.A." Developments in and the policies of other countries can have important effects on U.S. economic circumstances. Just as the recognition of new military vulnerabilities prompted a renaissance in thinking about military security during the Cold War, the recognition of new economic vulnerabilities and dependencies has started a new wave of thinking about economic security.

THE LIMITS OF THE NATIONAL-SECURITY METAPHOR

The analogy between the military challenges of the past and the economic challenges of today is a natural one. There *is* a strong element of competition in economic affairs. Markets won by Japanese firms are lost (at least for a time) to U.S. firms in the same industry. Sometimes the economic interests of nations *do* conflict. As military and political threats recede, attention has naturally focused on the potential threats posed by economic developments. Also, during an election year, casting potentially divisive questions of economic policy in the "us-against-them" language of national security has had obvious attractions. It should not be surprising that at least at the rhetorical level the emphasis during the last presidential campaign was less on "economic policy" than on "economic security."

We must exercise caution, though, in extending the metaphors of military security into the economic realm. Most of our thinking about the military aspects of national security is based on the analogy of warfare: When we win, someone else loses. In the military context, the most important situations to be dealt with are confrontational. In the military context, protecting U.S. national security interests almost always means protecting them *against* some foreign action. Advancing U.S. interests traditionally means acting *in the face of* foreign opposition.

But to limit our thinking about economics and national security to the confrontational framework that is characteristic of thinking about military security is to miss some of the most important elements of international economic relations. Unlike military activity, most economic activity is undertaken because it serves the interests of the parties involved. No international economic transaction involving Americans occurs unless it advances the interests of at least *some* Americans. Further, most economic activities are "positive-sum" in the sense that the net result of such activities is that more goods, more services, more income, etc., become available to the world at large. There is, of course, no guarantee that the additional output, income, or welfare will be distributed so as to make everybody better off; sometimes specific individuals, firms, communities, or nations will be made worse off. But still, economic activity typically results in there being more good things to be shared among competing interests. In this regard, economic activity stands in stark contrast to military (and perhaps political) activities, which almost inevitably consume or destroy resources, leaving less to go around. Economic activity provides at least the opportunity for all concerned to benefit. Military activity seldom does.[1]

Economic interactions among other countries may or may not advance U.S. interests, but there is no *a priori* reason to look upon such interactions as injurious to U.S. interests. They may just as well prove beneficial. While there might be arguments over particular incidents, few would suggest that the general increase in international economic activity since World War II has not been in the U.S. interest. Specific economic *events* may be inimical to U.S. interests, but international economic *activity* must be viewed as generally beneficial. To become preoccupied with potential economic threats is to risk ignoring potential economic opportunities. Only a policy of autarky will completely eliminate foreign economic threats to U.S. interests. But no one would argue that autarky is in the interests of the United States. True national security and the associated attention to U.S. national interests will require not just defending against economic threats but also recognizing and seizing economic opportunities. More often than not, seizing these opportunities will require cooperation with other nations rather than confrontation.

Another danger in extending the national security metaphor too glibly to economic matters is that it may lead to an excessive preoccupation with foreign developments, events, and actions. Traditional thinking about national security has focused on foreigners. It is the actions of *foreigners* (whether or not these actions are intentionally malicious) that threaten us and must therefore be countered. It is *foreign* interests that stand in the way of the United States achieving its aims. Of course, the possibility of internal or domestic threats to U.S. national security interests have always been recognized—spies, traitors, insurrection, and so on. Fortunately, though, internal threats to U.S. national security interests have been

---

[1]The exception may be military action of a deterrent or policing nature, which can make everybody better off, in the best of circumstances, by preserving peace and stability.

minor, and U.S. national security policy has been predominantly outward looking.

In the economic sphere, it may not be so easy to discount internal threats. Despite the increasingly international nature of the U.S. economy, the greatest threats to U.S. economic interests and capabilities are still home grown. Foreign economic actions or developments have never caused as much pain and anxiety within the U.S. population as have, for example, misjudged U.S. monetary and fiscal policies. No set of foreign trends or policies will affect the character and size of the U.S. economy as powerfully as do the domestic policies and attitudes that encourage or discourage saving, investment, and innovation. Neither does any foreign economic development pose as stark a threat to current and future U.S. prosperity as the failures to control health-care costs, to provide effective schooling for U.S. children, or to manage hazardous wastes. Protecting economic interests and capabilities from the negative consequences of domestic actions and developments is usually no less difficult and certainly no less important than protecting these same interests against external threats. An economic security policy that is exclusively, or even principally, outward looking will be seriously incomplete.[2]

USING ECONOMIC MEANS TO ACHIEVE NATIONAL SECURITY ENDS

A less remarked, but perhaps equally important, change in thinking about national security centers on the use of economic means to achieve traditional national-security ends. The collapse of the Soviet military threat allows the United States and its allies somewhat greater freedom in the use of military force. It is no longer necessary to worry as much about the potential escalation of a small-scale military intervention into a confrontation with a rival superpower. U.S. and allied willingness to commit troops in the Persian Gulf and in

---

[2]Having noted the inadequacy of an exclusively outward-looking economic security policy, we proceed in the rest of this report with a discussion that is mostly outward looking. We leave a discussion of the domestic aspects of economic prosperity to other authors not because these aspects are unimportant, but because they will be better treated by other authors in other contexts.

Somalia and debates over possible military interventions in Bosnia or in Haiti are reflections of this new freedom. At the same time, it is recognized that military action is not likely to be effective (and even less likely to be *cost*-effective, considering possible U.S. and allied losses) in pursuing some kinds of foreign-policy goals. Military force is sometimes effective in bringing about the ouster of an illegitimate or dangerous government, but it is a clumsy and probably inappropriate instrument, for example, for encouraging a return to democracy or adherence to U.S ideals of human rights. In an era when direct military action may become less frequent[3] and efforts to change the longer-term behavior of foreign governments and subnational groups may grow in importance, the United States may increasingly seek nonmilitary approaches to achieving its national security and foreign policy ends.

Often, the first responses to national security and foreign policy problems have been economic: trade restrictions, embargoes, freezing of financial assets, and so on. Military actions may follow, but economic policies often remain an important part of overall strategies. In some cases, economic actions may support or complement military action. Restrictions on shipments of militarily relevant supplies and equipment, for example, may weaken an opponent and increase the likelihood that subsequent military action will be successful. (Arguably, economic sanctions against Iraq had this effect.) In other cases, it is hoped that economic actions will turn out to be an effective substitute for military action. (Economic sanctions aimed at Serbia and Haiti are relevant examples here.) Sometimes, the economic elements of a strategy outlast the military aspects. The ultimate success of U.S. policy toward Panama, for example, may depend as much on the success of continuing U.S. efforts to rebuild the Panamanian economy as on the outcome of a brief military intervention.

The growing importance of economic measures as foreign policy tools confronts the traditional U.S. national-security establishment, and the military in particular, with a new set of policy problems. The traditional levers of economic policy are not always well suited to re-

---

[3]The experience of the early 1990s is not reassuring in this regard. One can hope, however.

sponding rapidly to foreign-policy and national-security demands. (Consider, for example, the difficulties encountered during the Iran hostage crisis in quickly identifying and freezing Iranian financial assets.) Governmental structures for planning and coordinating military and economic activities are often inadequate. Increasingly, the military is called upon to carry out missions for which it may not be adequately equipped or trained (monitoring commercial ship or air traffic, recognizing contraband cargoes, delivering humanitarian aid, etc.). Perhaps most importantly, no clear consensus has developed either within the national-security establishment or within the population at large about the relative effectiveness or utility of economic, as opposed to political or military, instruments in particular situations. Questions about whether and how best to combine economic measures with military and political ones have rarely been explicitly addressed. The result can be a confused and confusing debate (as we saw in connection with Iraq) about whether or not economic measures can or should substitute for more direct military action, how long to wait for economic measures to have an effect, and so on. More thought is needed about the respective roles of economic, political, and military tools for achieving national security objectives and about how to fashion these elements together into a larger national security policy.

THE PLAN OF THIS REPORT

In this report, we will address both of these "economic dimensions of national security": the increased importance of international economic events in shaping U.S. economic fortunes and the increased use of economic instruments for pursuing traditional foreign policy goals. Inevitably, the lines between the two will become blurred; foreign economic developments and actions can affect the United States' ability to employ economic measures to achieve foreign-policy objectives. Chapter Two of this report offers a definition of economic security and distinguishes the pursuit of economic security from the pursuit of more traditionally defined prosperity or economic well-being. Chapter Three discusses the pursuit of economic security through the pursuit of superior (to other countries) economic performance. Chapter Four suggests that economic security may require more than just keeping the U.S. economy and U.S. firms bigger, richer, or more productive than foreign economies and firms.

Chapter Five addresses the use of economic instruments to achieve national-security and foreign-policy ends. It deals with how we might define, recognize, and exercise "economic power." Chapter Six presents several concluding observations based on the preceding discussion.

Chapter Two

WHAT IS ECONOMIC SECURITY?

Despite all the talk about "economic security" that we have heard in recent years, no clear definition of what is meant by that phrase seems to have emerged. Economic affairs have, of course, always been a focus of public attention and public policy. Economic prosperity is among our most basic national interests. What, if anything, is new in the recent attention being paid to economic security? Does seeking economic security mean something different from the traditional desire for economic well-being? Is the pursuit of economic security operationally different from the pursuit of prosperity? Should new or different objectives be established for public policy—beyond those like economic growth, full employment, and low inflation that have always been pursued—to promote economic security?[1]

Although different people mean different things when they speak of economic security, two common threads seem to connect most of these references. The first is a concern with challenges, opposition, or uncertainty. Economic security is the ability to protect or to advance U.S. economic interests *in the face* of events, developments, or

---

[1]Some uncertainty on this point seems to reach to the very highest levels of the U.S. government. During the presidential campaign and during the immediate post-election period, candidate and then President-elect Clinton proposed the creation of an "Economic Security Council," advertised as a rough counterpart of the National Security Council, with responsibility for coordinating economic and economically relevant policies across government departments. By the time the new administration took office, the reference to security had been dropped from the name of the new "National Economic Council," although the function of the council had apparently not changed. Is there really any difference between a council concerned with economics and one concerned with economic security?

actions that may threaten or block these interests. These challenges or obstacles may be foreign or domestic in origin, intentional or accidental, and the consequences of human or natural forces. One of the objects of economic security is to reduce uncertainty about the continued economic well-being of the United States, to reduce the chances that its future economic well-being will fall below some (presumably ever-increasing) minimum acceptable level.

The second common thread is a concern with being able to shape the world to our liking and with being able to fend off challenges of a noneconomic nature. This will require, among other things, playing a major role in establishing the rules that govern international economic relations; making sure that the U.S. population gets what it thinks of as its rightful share of the global economic pie; influencing the policies—economic and otherwise—of other countries; and, not least, maintaining the economic wherewithal to support an adequate military.

The pursuit of economic security, then, encompasses efforts to protect U.S. economic prosperity (or some part of this prosperity) from loss and to shape the international economic and political-military environment to the advantage of most of the U.S. population.

Certainly, economic prosperity as usually defined—economic growth, full employment, low inflation, high levels of investment, improvements in productivity, etc.—will contribute to U.S. economic security. The best way to protect ourselves from the consequences of economic loss is to have lots to begin with. Also, the larger the U.S. presence in international markets is, the more it will be able to influence the rules under which those markets operate. The higher U.S. incomes are, the easier it will be for the United States to aid other countries, and (one hopes) thereby influence their policies. And, of course, national wealth and technological prowess make it possible to maintain large and capable armed forces.

But in some circumstances a desire for increased economic security will conflict with a desire for current prosperity. Sometimes it may be wise to sacrifice some current prosperity to make that of the future more stable, more certain, or less subject to loss. We may, for example, forgo opportunities to buy certain goods or services from low-cost foreign suppliers, because we think it important to encourage domestic production. (Goods essential to maintaining some military capabilities are the most obvious examples here.) Similarly, we may pass up chances for sales of certain products (arms, for example, or sophisticated computing equipment), because we prefer to keep these products out of certain hands. The government may raise taxes to fund public investments in infrastructure or in particular industries that it hopes will make U.S. incomes larger or more secure in the future. With the aim of enhancing social cohesion, the government may tax the most productive and successful members of the society (reducing perhaps their incentives to become yet more productive and successful) to assist the less productive or successful. As with any set of potentially or partially conflicting policy objectives, the pursuits of economic security and current prosperity will need to be continually balanced.[2]

In the following chapters of this report, we consider some specific ways in which the pursuit of economic security would seem to require something other than the simple pursuit of economic well-being. As a general rule, market forces will act to maximize the value of goods and services produced in the economy. There are exceptions to this general rule, of course, and government intervention in economic affairs is sometimes required. For the most part, though, market forces will be effective instruments for promoting prosperity. To the extent that economic security requires something other than maximizing the market value of goods and services produced, market forces may not be the most effective instruments for promoting economic security. Compiling a list, then, of factors or conditions other than simple prosperity that may contribute to economic security is at the same time to compile a list of objectives that may not be achieved through the operation of market forces alone. It has

---

[2]The pursuit of economic stability, certainty, and protection from loss—what we are calling here the pursuit of economic security—might alternatively be thought of as the pursuit of *long-run* prosperity, as opposed to the pursuit of *current* prosperity. The effective pursuit of long-term prosperity requires, after all, attention to the possibility of future instability, uncertainty, and loss—the same concerns that are central to the pursuit of economic security. Much has been written in recent years about the alleged failure of individual Americans, American firms, and American public institutions to show sufficient concern with the long run. The kinds of policies proposed by those who urge a longer-run view are often similar to the policies proposed by those advocating increased emphasis on economic security.

long been understood that the pursuit of military and political security requires direct government action. So, in many cases, will the pursuit of economic security.

Chapter Three

PURSUING ECONOMIC SECURITY

Much of the popular discussion of U.S. economic security focuses on the relative standing of the U.S. economy and of firms operating in the United States: Are they bigger, more productive, more innovative, etc., than foreign economies and firms operating abroad? Closely related are concerns about who controls important economic assets. Also prominent in the popular debate are questions about what is required to maintain U.S. military forces adequate to meet foreign challenges. Economic security, it seems, is naturally discussed today in terms of international competition and comparisons.

This focus on competition and comparisons reflects in part the habits we have learned in thinking about military security. Military security is inherently a competitive matter: The bigger, faster, or technologically superior force often wins. But there is more to this concern with relative standing than just habit. Some aspects of economic security really are advanced by being bigger, richer, more clever, or more productive or by exercising more control than someone else. In this section, we consider the pursuit of economic security through relative economic performance.

THE IMPORTANCE OF RELATIVE SIZE

In a recent book, Robert Reich recounts that for some time now he has been asking students "whether they would prefer living in a world in which every U.S. resident is 25 percent wealthier than now and every Japanese is much wealthier than the average U.S. resident, or in one in which U.S. residents are only 10 percent wealthier than now but ahead of the average Japanese."[1] He reports that a large number vote for the second option.

In the standard economic way of thinking, choosing the second option makes no sense. Why should the United States accept a sizable decrement in its standard of living just to be better off than the Japanese? For most purposes, it probably makes no difference whether U.S. residents are richer than Japanese; how much bigger the U.S. economy is than the Japanese economy; or who produces more cars, computers, or rice. We live in an integrated world economy. What is produced in Japan is typically available in the United States, and vice versa. If our principal concern is prosperity, what matters at the end of the day is what goods and services are available for us to consume or to invest in future production. The aim should be to maximize individual incomes, a measure of the total volume of goods and services one can command.

The fact that many Americans say they would be willing to sacrifice considerable income just to stay ahead of the Japanese is perhaps nothing more than a reflection of understandable (and not necessarily undesirable) national pride. We like to know that Americans are the biggest or the best, even if being so does nothing to make our lives immediately or materially better. It may also reflect, though, the perfectly rational realization that for some purposes there is a real advantage to being not just big or rich, but bigger or richer than somebody else. Later in this report, we will address the question of how to measure economic size and how these measurements relate to the economic instruments that can be utilized in support of national security policy.[2]

Who Makes the Rules?

Relative size is important, for example, when it comes to setting international rules. As a practical matter, the United States enjoys the power to veto any proposed agreement on international trading

---

[1]Robert B. Reich, *The Work of Nations*, Alfred A. Knopf, New York, 1991, p. 308.
[2]See Chapter Five.

rules. The United States is the world's largest trader,[3] and no general agreement on international trading rules would mean anything if it were not adhered to by the United States. As a consequence, the United States enjoys considerable leverage (at least of a negative sort) in shaping international trading rules. Recently, the United States has exercised this leverage to advance the economic interests of U.S. farmers, refusing to subscribe to a general trade agreement unless it includes limitations on foreign agricultural subsidies.

The countries of the European Union (EU), now acting as a unit for the purposes of trade negotiations, constitute an economic entity similar to the United States with regard to size and importance in world trade. As a unit, the EU too has the power to veto trade agreements, a power that none of its constituent countries enjoyed individually. Recently, the EU has exercised this power to defend the interests of its own farmers. The result was a prolonged impasse in the recent round of General Agreement on Tariffs and Trade (GATT) negotiations over the issue of farm subsidies.

It is easy to think of other cases in which simple size has allowed countries to make and to enforce rules of international economic behavior. Because it could easily expand its own production when necessary and because it was rich enough to absorb the financial consequences of reducing its output when necessary, Saudi Arabia was able for a decade to act as the world's swing producer of oil, setting world oil prices and maintaining production discipline within the Organization of Petroleum Exporting Countries (OPEC). Because the United States is such a large market for tuna, it has been able to demand that foreign tuna-fishing fleets use techniques that do not endanger dolphins. Being biggest or best in economic and industrial dimensions does sometimes help a country to get its way.

Relative size also provides obvious advantages in fielding military forces. The United States enjoys nearly unchallenged military supremacy in the world today, partly because no other nation comes

---

[3]In 1992, the United States accounted for 12 percent of total world merchandise exports and nearly 15 percent of total merchandise imports.

close to being able to match the resources the United States devotes to military activities.[4]

Rebuilding the European and Asian economies that had been devastated by World War II was, of course, a conscious objective of U.S. foreign and economic policy. The growth of these economies (and the algebraically inevitable relative diminishment of the U.S. economy) has served important U.S. interests. Economic recovery in Europe contributed to political and military stability there, which in turn allowed U.S. attention to be focused elsewhere. Japan and Western Europe served as clear demonstrations that capitalist and democratic systems could produce both robust economic growth and social equity. These rebuilt economies provided the economic underpinnings for powerful alliances that supported U.S. interests during the Cold War. Although differences that in the past were swept under the rug in the interests of alliance unity may now be more visible, the advanced industrialized and democratic nations continue to hold many interests in common. The United States can expect continuing support from Europe and Japan on many issues.

Today, the United States has an interest in promoting economic growth in the developing world and in formerly socialist countries— for the same sorts of reasons that it had an interest in rebuilding Europe and Japan. If the share of the world economy accounted for by the United States shrinks a bit further because its efforts to spur economic growth in these countries are successful, we should probably not be concerned. Few would argue that U.S. interests would have been better served if the U.S. economy stood today in the same relation to other economies that it did in, say, 1950.

As much as economic growth abroad has served and will continue to serve U.S. interests, the relative diminishment of the United States in economic terms has some negative consequences—for the United States and possibly for the world. By and large, the United States has been a benevolent and effective maker of international economic rules. International economic institutions and arrangements that were created as a result of U.S. economic leadership—for example, the World Bank, the International Monetary Fund, the GATT, the

---

[4]One could, of course, imagine alliances of nations that could field military forces comparable to our own, but this would require a good imagination.

Bretton Woods exchange-rate system—have served the world well. In some cases, the United States unilaterally preserved these institutions and arrangements—often simply by absorbing the consequences of other nations' deviations from agreed-upon rules. To some observers, it is not a coincidence that international cooperation in economic matters has become more problematic in recent years as U.S. economic dominance has become less pronounced. Witness the slow progress of the Uruguay Round of trade negotiations; squabbling about which countries' interest rates, budget deficits, or current account imbalances are too high or too large; difficulties in agreeing on global environmental standards; problems in sharing responsibility for assisting the reform of formerly socialist economies. If the United States will no longer be in a position to establish and enforce the international economic rules of the game, who will be? Will anybody be? And what reason is there to think that rules made jointly or by somebody else will be better—for the United States or for the world—than the rules that were made by the United States when it was more dominant economically than it is today? It is easy to understand why some observers—including some quite sophisticated ones—are less than completely comfortable with the prospect that the United States will account for a smaller share of the world economy.

Public and Private Size

Just as we derive some advantages from the relative size and wealth of the U.S. national economy, as a nation we may also derive advantages from the preeminence of some firms and enterprises operating in the United States.[5] Large firms, firms with large market shares,

---

[5]In today's environment, it makes more sense to speak of "firms operating in the United States" rather than "U.S. firms." For most public policy purposes, what we care about is whether a firm is supplying jobs locally, whether it is paying taxes locally, whether its output could be denied us in some international crisis, and so on. These are determined much more by the location of a firm's operations—where it does its manufacturing, where it keeps its inventories, where it does its research and development (R&D), etc.—than by where it is incorporated, where its headquarters building is, whether its name sounds American, what stock exchange its shares are traded on, or whatever other characteristic one might use to identify an "American firm." We also have an interest in who owns the firm—in who gets the profits. But today, ownership—at least of large firms whose shares are publicly traded—will not be confined to or perhaps even concentrated in any single country. In today's world, it makes little

firms that can produce at lower cost, or firms that possess superior technology or know-how may also enjoy some advantages in bargaining with other firms—with suppliers, with customers, or with competitors.[6] To the extent that advantaged firms are located in the United States and the firms they bargain with operate abroad, this bargaining leverage may yield net advantages for Americans in the form of higher wages, increased tax payments, or (if the owners are American) increased profits.

Staying Number One

We may, then, have a legitimate concern not only about how big or how rich (or how innovative, how resilient, how flexible, etc.) the U.S. economy and the enterprises that make it up are in absolute terms but also about how big or how rich (etc.) they are compared to other countries and other enterprises. Is it worth giving up 15 percent of U.S. gross domestic product (GDP) (to return to Reich's example) just to be ahead of the Japanese? Probably not. But is it worth giving up some smaller amount of consumption, using the resources for investment or to create an environment more conducive to successful economic activity, to maintain the United States as the world's economic leader? Possibly.

That the United States in recent years has been devoting a smaller share of GDP to saving and investment and a larger share to consumption than have other industrialized nations is a widely noted fact. National saving and investment rates in 1990, for example, are shown in Table 1.

In one sense, this should not be a cause for concern. The division of national income between current consumption and investment for the future reflects individual and collective preferences for current versus future income. Aggregate levels of saving and consumption are the results of decisions by individual households and firms and of collective decisions regarding government budget policies. No out-

---

sense to try to attach a national label to large firms with shareholders, workers, managers, and operations scattered around the world.

[6]None of these attributes *ensures* either a competitive or a bargaining advantage, of course. It is not hard to think of large firms, for example, that have fared poorly in recent years.

Table 1

Saving and Investment in Industrialized Countries, 1990
(as percentages of GDP)

	National Saving	Gross Fixed Capital Formation
United States	14.3	17.0
Canada	18.0	21.5
Japan	34.4	32.6
Germany	25.0	21.4
France	21.1	22.1
Italy	19.5	20.7
United Kingdom	15.6	19.2
European Union	21.2	21.4

SOURCES: OECD and IMF

NOTE: These 1990 rates are roughly characteristic for the entire decade of the 1980s.

side power is forcing U.S. residents to consume rather than save. They are saving—at least roughly—as much as they want to save.

But if current patterns of consumption, saving, and investment are maintained, economic growth in the United States will almost certainly be slower than growth in much of the rest of the industrialized world, and the relative size of the U.S. economy will decline yet further. If the relative size does contribute to economic security (and we have argued that it does), then the pursuit of economic security provides a rationale for encouraging saving and investment in areas that will contribute to the longer-term growth of the U.S. economy. Proposed actions to achieve these ends are numerous: Reduce government spending for current consumption; increase government spending for infrastructure investment; raise taxes to reduce government deficits and to curtail private consumption; change tax laws to encourage private saving and investment; discourage investment in "nonproductive" assets, such as housing; encourage investment in R&D, plant and equipment, and education and training; and so on. A consensus in favor of policies to increase saving and investment in the United States—necessarily at the expense of some current consumption—seems to be forming. (There is, of course, still heated debate over precisely what or whose current consumption should be sacrificed to achieve this end.) In part, this increased national interest in saving and investment reflects a changing assessment of the relative worth of current versus future consumption—a growing suspicion that if more is not invested today, U.S. living standards may be unacceptable in the future. But it also reflects a growing concern about the relative place of the United States in the world economy. As Reich's anecdote suggests, Americans do see value in being number one, and they appear to be willing to make some sacrifices to retain this ranking.

More technically, the potential benefits that stem from the relative size of the U.S. economy are true public goods. Most U.S. residents stand to benefit, for example, from the leverage in international negotiations that relative size creates, whether or not they have individually contributed to maintaining this relative size.[7] As a result, private incentives to engage in the kinds of activities—saving and investment, for example—that will make the economy grow will not bring about the optimal level of such activities. In fulfilling its responsibility to promote the public interest, then, governments should arguably take steps—in the allocation of public spending, the design of tax policies, etc.—to encourage higher levels of saving, investment, education, R&D, and other activities that will contribute to national economic growth than will grow out of purely private decisionmaking.

Beyond trying to spur economic growth in the United States, should we also seek to slow the growth of other nations? In rare situations, perhaps. From time to time, the U.S. government has adopted policies aimed specifically at retarding the economic growth of other nations. We maintain restrictions on economic dealings with a few countries (Iraq, Cuba, Libya, North Korea, and Serbia, for example). Partly, these restrictions are meant to provide leverage for influencing the behavior of these countries: Cooperate and we will ease this or that restriction.[8] Principally, though, restrictions are intended to weaken the target economies and hasten the downfall of regimes considered undesirable.

---

[7]Assuming, perhaps optimistically, that U.S. negotiators use this leverage wisely enough to generate benefits for most of the U.S. population.

[8]We take up the use of economic means to achieve traditional policy ends in more detail in Chapter Five.

It seems improbable, though, that the U.S. government would ever seek actively to undermine the general economy of any more-or-less friendly nation or to hinder specific firms operating there. In most cases, doing so would threaten its own interests. If the target country were large, the United States might risk retaliation. More important, U.S. producers would likely suffer as less-prosperous foreigners bought fewer U.S.-made goods. U.S. consumers, too, would suffer if foreign-made goods were not as available or as attractive as they might have been. In general, U.S. prosperity is enhanced by the prosperity of other countries.

As a practical matter, concerns over relative size and relative standing in particular markets or industries will motivate government policies designed not so much to hinder foreign economic activity as to promote or encourage U.S. activity. We may note, for example, that foreign producers are outpacing U.S. producers in particular industries, and therefore consider government assistance for U.S. firms in these same industries.[9] Similarly, the recognition that other economies are investing a larger share of their incomes than U.S. residents are and may therefore be expected to grow more rapidly in coming years may spur us to change tax laws or government spending programs to encourage more saving and investment. For the most part, then, more rapid growth in other countries should be seen as creating examples to be considered and possibly to be emulated rather than targets to be attacked.

SUPPORT FOR SPECIFIC INDUSTRIES

No one doubts the importance of government efforts to make the overall economic climate more conducive to investment, innovation, productivity improvements, and economic growth. Policies to reduce government deficits, boost domestic saving, create more highly skilled work forces, encourage entrepreneurial risk taking, etc., are on nearly everybody's lists of What Governments Ought To Be Doing. Much more controversial, however, are government efforts to provide special support for or to promote the growth of particular industries.

---

[9]We discuss below the difficulty of identifying circumstances that may justify such assistance.

We have heard much in recent years about the potential benefits and dangers of "industrial policies" and "strategic trade policies" (the names commonly attached to efforts to promote the fortunes of particular industries in, respectively, domestic and international markets). Governmental support for the European Airbus consortium and Japanese support for the supercomputer and semiconductor industries are cited variously as models of effective government pursuit of national economic interests, as serious threats to the international trading order, and as ineffective wastes of taxpayers' money. Similarly, the alleged failure of the U.S. government to provide support or protection for "key" U.S. industries is seen alternatively as a dismal shirking of governmental responsibility, a wise refusal by the government to get involved in matters better left to private decisionmakers, or a complete misunderstanding of what the U.S. government is really doing. Some argue that the combination of (alleged) foreign activism and (alleged) U.S. government inaction threatens the international competitiveness of firms operating in the United States and that U.S. economic interests—and therefore U.S. economic security—will suffer as a result. Others argue that increased government support for particular industries—governmental "picking of winners and losers" is how such efforts are often characterized by opponents—will only slow the growth of the U.S. economy, risk setting off international disputes about what constitutes "fair" support for particular industries, and therefore itself constitute a threat to U.S. economic security. There is wide agreement, though, that policies adopted by one nation to support specific industries or economic activities will often have consequences for other nations. Consequently, a workable strategy for promoting U.S. economic security must include some notion of when the U.S. government should provide assistance to specific industries and when it should oppose similar actions by other governments.

More precisely, policymakers must come to grips with four basic questions: When does the pursuit of U.S. economic interests require government support for particular industries? Can such support be effectively provided, and if so, how? In what circumstances will foreign support for particular industries threaten U.S. interests? And how can the U.S. government best counter undesirable policies by foreign governments? We deal with each of these questions in turn.

When Is Special Support Justified?

One possible justification for government support for a particular industry is the presence of significant economies of scale. A firm or an industry is said to exhibit economies of scale if, once some minimum level of operations is achieved, succeeding increments to output come at lower cost—if it is cheaper to produce the one-thousandth copy of an item than the one-hundredth, cheaper to make the one-millionth than the ten-thousandth, and so on. Economies of scale are most likely to be found in industries where large up-front investments in production facilities, R&D, distribution network development, etc., are required before large-scale production is possible. The longer the production run over which these initial costs can be amortized, the lower the average cost of all the units produced. The belief is widespread (although not fully substantiated yet by careful analysis) that economies of scale are particularly characteristic of modern, high-technology, research-intensive industries. Certainly, though, some older, "smoke-stack" industries—autos, steel, and shipbuilding come immediately to mind—also show significant economies of scale.

The significance of economies of scale lies in the fact that a firm that captures an early market share may be the first to achieve efficient scale and may therefore enjoy a significant cost advantage over competitors stuck at lower rates of production. This advantage may allow the leading firm to undersell its competition and to capture an even larger share of the market, which may in turn create an even greater cost advantage, and so on. None of the steps in this chain happens automatically, of course, and there is no guarantee that capturing a large share of the early market for a product will allow a firm to dominate its industry. Neither are the competitive advantages that arise from large-scale production necessarily permanent; it is easy to think of firms that once enjoyed significant cost advantages and came to dominate their industries, only to be surpassed by a new or particularly hard-charging competitor. Nonetheless, in industries where economies of scale are important, capturing a large market share can yield significant competitive advantages.

What makes economies of scale relevant to considerations of economic security is that economic advantages may accrue to the nation whose firms can capture market share and the attendant competitive advantages. Firms may enjoy larger profits. Wages for workers may rise. Tax revenues may increase. Governments may, therefore, have an interest—some would say a responsibility—to do what they can to help firms that operate locally (rather than firms that operate principally in other countries) to capture economies of scale.

Assistance may take the form of direct subsidies for R&D or for production, which will allow firms to cut prices and gain market share. (Airbus, for example, is gaining international market share as a consequence of government subsidies.) Alternatively, support could come in the form of large public-sector purchases that will help establish efficient-scale operations. (This is the classic "infant industry" policy: Support an infant until it is strong enough to stand on its own. The U.S. aerospace industry is widely thought to have been helped by large government purchases of military systems.) Finally, support may take the form of restrictions on imports so that the home-country firm can rely on a secure domestic market as a base on which to build total market share. (Japan is frequently accused of adopting such policies.)

Nothing comes free, of course. Special assistance for particular firms or industries necessarily comes at a cost to consumers or to other industries. These costs may be either direct (taxes to finance subsidies) or indirect (higher prices for imported goods or higher interest rates if subsidies are financed by government borrowing), but they will certainly be real. The simple fact that industries targeted for special assistance do in fact achieve a competitive advantage over foreign firms does not suffice to prove that the government programs that promoted this outcome were effective or worthwhile. A complete accounting of the value of government intervention must include consideration of what happened to industries and interests *not* target for special assistance and of what might reasonably have been expected to happen in the absence of intervention.[10]

---

[10]In the 1960s and 1970s, the Japanese government aggressively supported the growth of the Japanese steel industry. Japanese steel producers did in fact capture a very large share of the world steel market, but subsequent analyses have shown that the gains that accrued to the Japanese economy from this competitive victory were less than the returns that could have been expected if the resources used to promote the steel industry had been left in the hands of private investors. In retrospect, it appears that the government program did more harm than good. See Paul R. Krugman, "Targeted

Special support for industries or firms may also be justified if the actions or activities of one industry or firm will provide important benefits for other industries and firms. These benefits might take the form of transfers of special skills or technical know-how that are facilitated by proximity. Technical know-how that is embodied in the knowledge and skills of individual workers, for example, may be transferred from one firm to another as workers leave one job and take another. This job changing and the associated technical cross-fertilization will arguably be more frequent if a number of firms employing similar kinds of workers are located close together, so that changing jobs does not require selling a house, uprooting a family, etc. Similarly, technical know-how may spread through casual contacts among workers in different firms. Such mechanisms may create a "beehive effect" whereby a number of similar firms located close together mutually support each other. The common example of such an agglomeration of similar firms is California's Silicon Valley.[11]

On a larger scale, one might hypothesize that "local" spillovers of technical know-how extend as far as an entire country. Despite rapidly improving communication, some kinds of know-how can be transmitted effectively only through direct personal contact. Direct consultation and movements of workers are, of course, much easier when there is no need to cross national, cultural, and linguistic boundaries. Thus, it is conceivable that governments have an interest in promoting the sorts of industries that create or rely on know-how of a sort that is not easily transmitted impersonally. Technological innovations relevant to such industries that are made abroad may not be as available, for example, to U.S. firms as would be similar innovations made in the United States. The United States might, then, prefer that these innovations be made here and therefore may wish to encourage the kinds of activity that would generate innovation.

Industrial Policies: Theory and Evidence," in Dominick Salvatore, ed., *The New Protectionist Threat to World Welfare*, North-Holland, 1987.

[11]Silicon Valley, however, is a classic example of a strongly self-reinforcing industrial complex that arose *without* any intentional government assistance. Although it is a valid theoretical proposition that government assistance *could* make other Silicon Valleys more likely, it is hard to see how targeted government assistance could have improved the original.

A related concern has to do with access to new and emerging technologies and products. Almost by definition, information about new technologies and products will be imperfect. It takes time for information to spread; information about new products will not be as fully disseminated as information about older, more established products. There is presumably some advantage in getting information about new products and technologies earlier rather than later; other products can be designed, for example, to take advantage of capabilities that will be offered by an about-to-be-marketed component. To the extent that information about new capabilities and designs spreads first to other firms that are "local" in geographical, cultural, or linguistic senses, there may be a justification for government efforts to encourage the "local" (i.e., in this country) establishment of the firms expected to produce new and more capable components.

The fact that the output of an industry serves as an input to other industries is not, in itself, a justification for special support. One cannot argue, for example, that, simply because many industries in the United States use steel, special support should be provided for the steel industry or that, because the computer industry requires lots of semiconductors, the chip industry should be promoted. To make a case for special support, it is also necessary to argue that the benefits generated by an industry are not fully captured by firms in that industry and are therefore not taken fully into account when decisions are made about production levels. Only when a market failure of some sort can be demonstrated—a failure of the full costs and benefits of some activity to be felt by those engaging in it—is there even a chance of making a credible case for special government support.[12] Similarly, arguments that an industry is likely to show rapid growth in the future are not sufficient to justify special support. Again, it must be demonstrated that prices charged and paid in market transactions will systematically fail to reflect the true value of the output.

---

[12]The standard case for government support of R&D efforts, for example, rests on the assertion that the full benefits of R&D activity cannot be captured by the firm doing the R&D. Despite patent protection and licensing arrangements, other firms are likely to share in the benefits generated by technological innovations. Since some of the benefits are likely to available for free, firms may be tempted to let someone else perform the expensive and risky R&D. Without some additional encouragement in the form of government support, the result is likely to be lower levels of R&D activity than would be justified by the total benefits resulting from such activity.

Practical Problems

The logic of the above arguments for governmental support of certain industries is well established and widely accepted. Applying this logic to particular cases, however, has proved exceedingly difficult. Arguments in favor of special support for particular industries must usually be prospective in nature: If scale is increased, costs are *expected* to come down; if costs come down, a firm is *expected* to capture a greater market share; if the firm gains a larger market share, benefits are *expected* in the form of higher profits, higher wages, or increased tax revenues; technical know-how is *expected* to be transmitted among firms without compensation to the originating firm when it will be valuable to other firms. The government also must project the consequences of intervention: It must believe in advance that subsidies or protection from foreign competition will in fact generate the economies of scale or the positive externalities that are theoretically possible. It is also necessary to believe that actions by one government to promote the growth of certain of its industries will not be countered by actions by another government seeking to support its own industries.[13] All of this is necessarily speculative. That the net social benefits arising out of special support for selected industries will outweigh the costs of such support is by no means easy to establish in specific cases.

Even with the benefit of hindsight, it is difficult to establish that government support for particular industries has been worth the cost. (It is always hard to know what would have happened in the absence of special government support.) The result is that we simply do not know how often the circumstances that will allow beneficial government intervention do in fact arise, or how long we can expect benefits generated by government intervention to last before other governments take actions to capture similar benefits for their own firms. In the absence of clear evidence—either prospectively or retrospectively—that government support for specific industries can be

---

[13]Intentionally or otherwise, large-volume purchases of aircraft by the U.S. government may have provided an important boost for U.S. engine and airframe manufacturers. The subsidies being poured into the Airbus consortium by European governments appear to be eroding the advantages previously enjoyed by the U.S. aerospace industry.

beneficial, some skepticism about such support is probably warranted.[14]

Because it is so hard to base decisions about government support for specific industries on verifiable fact, such decisions must inevitably be based to a large degree on opinion. And when opinion serves as the basis for government decisionmaking, the door is opened for special pleading by every industry to which the arguments for special support might plausibly apply.

In the face of such difficulties and to preserve some appearance of objectivity and freedom from special pleading, it has become common in the last few years to appoint blue-ribbon panels, commissions, or committees charged with identifying "critical technologies" deserving of special care and support.[15] Typically, these panels, commissions, and committees have been rather vague in specifying the criteria by which technologies are judged to be critical.[16] None, to our knowledge, has specifically recognized the centrality of market failure as the indicator that government action is necessary or potentially valuable. For the most part, they have concentrated their efforts on forecasting which technologies will show the most rapid

---

[14]Some skepticism is warranted also with regard to governmental actions aimed at making the overall economic climate more conducive to investment, innovation, increases in productivity, and economic growth. These actions—reducing government deficits, encouraging education and training, adjusting product liability laws, regulating capital markets, and so on—typically impose costs on somebody, and we must of course ask whether the benefits of these actions really do outweigh their costs. The preference that many economists show for general rather than industry- or sector-specific policies seems to arise from a sense (as opposed to a clearly demonstrable fact) that the task of making general policy is somehow simpler and more likely to be accomplished successfully than that of making policy to aid a specific industry or sector. (At the very least, there is no need to choose which industry or sector to support.)

[15]Since the late 1980s, more than a dozen lists of "critical technologies" have been generated in the United States. The sponsors of critical-technology lists have included the Department of Defense (DoD), the Department of Commerce, the White House-organized National Critical Technology Panels, the private-sector Council on Competitiveness, and organizations representing the aerospace and computer industries.

[16]They have also been vague about defining just what constitutes a "technology." A quick survey of these lists reveals some confusion about whether support is being proposed for "technologies," "industries," "industrial sectors," or branches of "science." A possibly apocryphal but accurate characterization of critical-technology lists to date is that they can include everything from "physics to batteries." We are grateful to our RAND colleague Bruce Bimber for this telling anecdote.

development in coming years or which will contribute most importantly to lower production costs in a variety of industries.[17] These considerations are not entirely irrelevant to the search for market failures, but the final step of actually trying to identify specific cases where markets will incorrectly value products seems not to have been taken.

The lists of critical technologies that have resulted from these exercises have typically been very broad, seemingly excluding few technologies. If the recommendations of these panels were acted upon, the resulting policies would amount to generalized support for all R&D rather than special help for a few selected industries. General assistance is almost certainly the preferable course, and the panels and commissions may ultimately have served a useful function, even if unwittingly.

When Are Foreign Industrial Policies Contrary to U.S. Interests?

But these are the cautions of academics. Despite the flimsiness of the case in favor of government support for particular industries, governments all over the world have embarked on policies of aggressive support for favored industries. Do such policies threaten U.S. interests? In some cases, obviously not. Efforts by the government of Brazil, to pick an extreme example, to increase the productivity of Brazilian coffee growers will likely benefit U.S. consumers and are unlikely to do serious harm to any other domestic interest, since the United States has no coffee-growing industry. European subsidies for grain growers and Japanese subsidies and protection for rice producers, however, may be an entirely different story. When should the United States be concerned about foreign industrial policies?

The United States should resist or seek to counter foreign industrial policies whenever there is a real prospect that these efforts may cre-

---

[17]These are among the more sensible criteria advanced. Some efforts to identify critical technologies have focused on the contribution of particular technologies to job growth or to reducing the trade deficit. Employment levels and external balances, of course, are determined principally by macroeconomic policies and conditions and are not influenced importantly by developments in specific sectors of the economy.

ate a foreign monopoly that will one day allow foreigners to collect monopoly profits from the U.S. population.[18] Dominance in a particular industry by producers operating in a single foreign country may also heighten somewhat the risk that U.S. buyers may face supply interruptions in a time of international crisis. In practice, we should probably view with suspicion any foreign subsidy to industries that might plausibly show significant economies of scale.

The United States should also resist foreign subsidies that may displace U.S. producers in world markets without bringing any price reductions for U.S. consumers. Foreign agricultural subsidies, for example, are damaging to U.S. interests, because they allow subsidized foreign farmers to capture third-country markets that might otherwise have been won by U.S. growers. Because U.S. government programs place a floor under prices for many farm commodities in the United States, foreign subsidies generally do little to reduce costs faced by U.S. consumers. Thus, as a result of foreign subsidies, U.S. producers lose and U.S. consumers do not gain—a situation that is clearly counter to overall U.S. interests.

The situation is more complicated when foreign policies do benefit U.S. consumers. If there is reason to believe that the benefits that accrue to consumers are only temporary and will evaporate if and when U.S. or other producers are driven from the market, the United States should of course oppose the foreign efforts to support a particular industry. But clear examples of such predation—cutting prices long enough to drive competitors out of business and then raising prices—are hard to identify, and one might reasonably be suspicious about the likely success of alleged predatory policies. More frequently, policymakers will have to weigh the benefits that accrue to U.S. consumers against the costs borne by U.S. producers as a consequence of foreign policies of industrial support. Making such assessments will never be easy, of course, but it would certainly be wrong to conclude that any foreign policy that threatens or appears to threaten U.S. producers is automatically contrary to broader U.S. interests. If foreign taxpayers are indirectly providing a subsidy

---

[18]This monopoly position might be achieved immediately—as when foreign firms come to dominate an emerging market—or at some later date when subsidized foreign production may eventually succeed in driving competitors out of business, thus creating a future monopoly.

to U.S. consumers, sometimes the right policy course will be to re-main silent and to enjoy the good fortune.

A Special Role for the United States?

The above arguments have a troublingly asymmetrical character: It might be advantageous for the United States to subsidize or other-wise encourage industries that show economies of scale. At the same time, it should be suspicious when other countries do likewise. In the military sphere, of course, the United States is used to taking ac-tions (building forces, etc.) that it would correctly view as threatening if undertaken by another country. But it has also long recognized that its security can be enhanced if all nations forswear certain ac-tions. A similar case might be made with regard to industrial or technological subsidies and assistance.

As the world's largest economy, the United States does have a special role to play in setting the standard for correct international economic behavior. Resisting the temptation to capture an international ad-vantage for a single U.S. industry is not necessarily an act of idealis-tic naiveté. If the United States openly pursues advantages for its own industries at whatever cost to the rest of the world, it is hard to imagine what arguments could be advanced in favor of restraint in other countries. The mechanisms for governmental intervention in economic affairs are, fortunately, poorly developed in the United States compared to most other nations. There is little reason to be-lieve that a world in which all governments worked hard to capture a special advantage for their own industries would be a world that would favor U.S. interests, either absolutely or relatively.

This is not to argue that U.S. restraint from aggressive rent-seeking industrial policy will necessarily foster similar restraint worldwide. (That *would* be naive.) It is to suggest, though, that if the United States does not show such restraint, few other countries are likely to do so. U.S. restraint with respect to tariffs and competitive ex-change-rate devaluations during the past 50 years has contributed to at least a rough international rejection of the most blatant beggar-thy-neighbor policies. The result has been an expansion of world trade that has benefited the United States. Perhaps U.S. leadership with respect to industrial subsidies will have a similarly salubrious effect.

We might go a step further, to turn some of the arguments common today on their heads. It has long been recognized that in some instances government subsidies or other assistance to particular industries is desirable. In the right circumstances, such assistance can improve overall welfare. But why should U.S. taxpayers clamor for the U.S. government to spend their taxes to produce what may be a worldwide public good? Consider, for example, biomedical research. Considerable sums of U.S. tax dollars support advanced biomedical research. The benefits of this research reach patients all over the world, patients who have contributed nothing to its pursuit. Rather than demanding further U.S. government support for biomedical research on the strength of the dubious assumption that this support will somehow maintain the primacy of some U.S.-based pharmaceutical or medical equipment firms, should we not instead be calling for other governments to pay their fair share? We have become accustomed to the notion that the burdens of common defense must be shared. Why not international burdensharing for biomedical research? But if it comes to that, why not ask other nations to share in the cost of producing a nonpolluting car or better communication technologies?

Protecting U.S. Interests

Although we may have doubts about whether policies designed to promote particular industries will ultimately prove beneficial for the countries adopting them, there is no question that these policies can damage the interests of firms and workers in other countries. It will be no consolation to U.S. workers who have lost jobs or firms that have been driven out of business because of foreign subsidies to learn years later that these subsidies did more harm than good to the foreign economies that offered them. Clearly, the pursuit of U.S. economic security will on occasion require action to discourage aggressive subsidization or protection of particular industries.

Fighting fire with fire and instituting a U.S. policy of industrial support is not obviously the best course. To borrow an analogy from thinking about military security, industrial subsidization and protection are similar to building military forces. The United States may gain a temporary advantage over other countries if it subsidizes more heavily than they do. But if other countries respond by offering yet more support for their own industries, the U.S. advantage is eroded. In the extreme, the United States could see the commercial equivalent of an arms race. Government support for a few industrial sectors thought to be key for future economic success would grow continually; economies would become more and more distorted as resources were poured into these "strategic" industries; and at the end of the day, because each move had been countered by foreign responses, no country would have much to show for its efforts.

The United States has learned through years of military competition that it is sometimes desirable or necessary to engage in arms races, principally to convince an adversary that the United States will do whatever is necessary to counter policies it views as detrimental to its interests. If this adversary is convinced that it is impossible to gain a lasting advantage, the temptation to seek an advantage may be lessened or removed. Much better, though, for all countries concerned to agree not to embark on an arms race in the first place. Perhaps this way of thinking should become more common with regard to commercial matters, with the major industrialized nations mutually agreeing to forswear specifically targeted programs of industrial support and concentrating instead on creating a general economic climate that is conducive to growth.

Another useful policy lesson may be drawn from our experience with military competition. In the military sphere, countries often seek to build their military capabilities first in those areas where they believe themselves to have a strong natural advantage. It is often unwise for another country to attempt to counter this kind of build-up directly; to do so would be to agree to play a game in which one's opponent enjoys an advantage. The collapse of the Soviet Union, for example, may have been hastened by the Soviet decision to engage in an extremely costly attempt to compete with U.S. R&D in advanced military technologies, where the United States enjoyed a clear technological advantage. A better course is often for other countries to counter the original build-up indirectly, concentrating on the things that they do best and hoping for a chance someday to trade reductions in unlike systems. Rather than seeking to match the massive armored forces of the Warsaw Pact, for example, the NATO allies sought to create effective anti-tank weapons.

The analogy to international commercial policy lies in the question
of whether it is typically a wise policy to counter foreign industrial
subsidies and support with subsidies and support in the same industries. In building military forces, the ultimate objective is not always
to have bigger military forces. Sometimes, it is to discourage other
nations from building bigger military forces. Similarly, in the commercial sphere, the ultimate objective should not be to subsidize a
particular U.S. industry as heavily as its foreign competition is subsidized. Instead, the aim should be to discourage foreign subsidies.
This aim may not always be most effectively achieved by countering
foreign subsidies directly with U.S. subsidies in the same industry.
Although a policy of direct confrontation will sometimes be required,
a preferable course may be to respond with support for some other
industry. If the Japanese are already using public funds to support
Japanese makers of, say, memory chips, the prospects that a U.S.
government response will prove beneficial may be increased if it is
concentrated in an industry where prices are not already being de-
pressed by forced expansion of foreign production. If the main purpose of U.S. industrial support is to create a bargaining chip (as
opposed to a microelectronic one) that will encourage foreign
governments to give up their own subsidy programs, then we may be
well advised to create this chip in an industry where U.S. producers
already enjoy some advantage.[19]

MAINTAINING AN ADEQUATE MILITARY

With the collapse of the Soviet empire and the end of the Cold War,
the military threats confronting the United States have clearly declined. The world remains a dangerous place, however, and sometimes the only way to protect or to advance U.S. national interests—
economic or otherwise—is through the application of military force.
Although presumably needing a smaller military today than in the
recent past, the United States will have to maintain substantial and
highly capable military forces for the foreseeable future.

---

[19]Such subsidization may engender awkward political problems. How will we choose
which industry is lucky enough to become our bargaining chip and receive the
associated subsidy? Perhaps one of the attractions of meeting a foreign subsidy with a
matching subsidy in the same industry is that such a policy apparently (but not, of
course, really) spares U.S. policymakers from having to make tricky choices.

Military strength, of course, requires an economic underpinning. The most basic requirement is that the United States maintain a level of general economic output that allows diversion of some resources to military uses. The collapse of the Soviet Union as a military superpower provides a stark example of how general economic failure can defeat even the most determined national-defense efforts. In a democracy, the effects of poor economic performance on the ability to maintain military capability will typically be more subtle but no less real. Sluggish economic performance will result in increased competition for available resources and pressure to reduce "unnecessary" defense spending so that resources can be used for other purposes. Robust economic growth will not eliminate all opposition to defense spending, of course, but the prospects for ensuring that adequate resources are devoted to the defense effort must certainly be improved when output is expanding rapidly and more resources are available for all purposes.

Fostering Technological Innovation

At a more microeconomic level, maintaining an effective military may be easier or more certain if some specific industrial capabilities are maintained. Perhaps prime among these will be the capability to design and to produce successive generations of technologically sophisticated weapons. Throughout the Cold-War era, U.S. military doctrine and the U.S. military posture have reflected a reliance on technologically sophisticated weaponry. In some cases, technological sophistication was necessary to offset the superior numbers of enemy forces (as in the Cold War confrontations with the Warsaw Pact). This was a wise choice, given U.S. capabilities relative to other nations, to produce quality versus quantity. U.S. reliance on technology also reflects an understandable reluctance to risk U.S. lives in pursuit of military goals. Much better to use fewer soldiers and more equipment. For these same reasons, a reliance on technological superiority in the military sphere will remain a sound strategy for the foreseeable future.

Technical superiority in the military sphere should probably extend over presumed allies, as well as over potential adversaries. Politics sometimes changes more rapidly than technology, and today's technologically sophisticated ally may become tomorrow's technologically sophisticated adversary—before a new generation of military hardware can be designed, built, and deployed. And it will always be easier to control the spread of advanced weapon systems if they are produced in the United States. Even steadfast allies may occasionally have ideas different from those of the United States about which other countries can be permitted access to sophisticated weaponry. More broadly, maintaining the technical superiority of U.S. military systems will probably yield some political leverage. If other nations must come to the United States to gain access to the most capable weapon systems in the world, they may be more inclined to conform their actions to U.S. wishes.

Even when U.S. technology appears to be superior to that found elsewhere, it will be prudent for U.S. arms makers to continue to innovate and improve. Technological progress, particularly militarily relevant technological progress, is not always apparent. As more and more countries gain the technological sophistication to build highly capable weapon systems, the need to protect against technological surprise becomes more pressing. Also, if U.S. forces enjoy a clear technological advantage over the forces of other nations, and if the U.S. defense industrial base is recognized as being able to maintain this lead, other nations may be deterred from mounting efforts to surpass the technological capabilities of U.S. forces.

But how is the United States to pursue this technological superiority? One approach is to try to identify those particular technologies that are key to the ability to field superior military equipment and then to provide through government channels whatever support is required to keep the United States ahead of other countries in these areas. Behind this approach is the realization that the United States today is not, cannot be, and should not attempt to be the international leader in all technological areas. Instead, the United States should target its resources on those technological areas where foreign superiority might prove militarily troublesome.

But how to do this? It is far from clear that compiling, *ex ante*, lists of especially worthy or promising technologies and then trying to foster their development is really the most fruitful way to pursue militarily relevant technical superiority. First, there are severe analytical difficulties in trying to define which technologies are really critical to the production of sophisticated weaponry. It is not unduly uncharitable to characterize the lists of critical technologies compiled to date as representing little more than a consensus of intuitions among people experienced in the design of modern weapon systems. In none of these cases have clear and objective criteria for "criticality" been proposed and applied. Perhaps no such criteria can be devised. Second, providing government support for specific kinds of research or for specific industrial processes is issuing an invitation for special pleading. Claims that one or another technology is essential to preserving the military might of the United States will become the last (and in some cases the first) refuge of every industrial special interest. Government agencies have not distinguished themselves in the past by being able to resist such claims. Third, having once identified a critical technology, there is still the problem of deciding what kind of government action will in fact encourage innovation. Simply providing financial support is not always adequate or even helpful.

Finally, relying on government agencies to identify and to support critical technologies may impart an unwanted conservative bias to technology policy. A public institution distributing public funds will have to document its reasons for acting as it does. Establishing a clear rationale for supporting technologies that do not yet exist or are in only the earliest stages of their developments will inevitably be difficult. Further, the people most closely associated with nascent technologies and possessing the clearest understanding of what these technologies may be able to achieve may be relative newcomers and less likely than experts in better established technologies to have the professional stature, the kinds of track records, and (more cynically) the political clout necessary to be appointed to governmental advisory panels. For both reasons, advisory panels and government agencies may have a tendency to err on the side of established technologies rather than take a gamble on something less certain. Yet it is precisely the latter sort of technologies that may provide the greatest return for a modest investment of public money. These may also be the technologies for which it is most difficult to attract commercial financing. By trying to identify particular technology areas as worthy of special support, one may end up placing one's bets on the technologies of the present rather than those of the future.

An alternative approach to choosing specific technologies as particularly critical is creating a general environment that will foster inno-

vation in the defense industrial base. It has been only in the last few
years that serious attention has been turned to understanding the
process by which sophisticated weapon systems are designed and
built. There is still considerable controversy over which steps in this
process are truly critical. Is it, perhaps, quite acceptable for basic
scientific and technological progress to be spread around the world
as long as the United States retains the skilled engineering design
teams that can combine scientific and engineering know-how to
create a new generation of sophisticated military equipment? Or can
these design teams function effectively only if they maintain close
contact with bench scientists and component designers, so that they
can anticipate innovations and incorporate the very latest advances?
If the latter, is the necessary contact possible if innovations and new
components are being developed abroad? And if we are convinced
that some kinds of basic research must be done here, how can government policies encourage the necessary research? Can military
acquisition policies be adjusted so as to encourage more innovation
or to make better use of innovations generated in the civilian economy? Most important of all, is it useful to think about designing
policies specifically to encourage innovation in the defense-goods
sector, or is militarily relevant innovation achieved reliably only if the
entire economy is good at generating innovation? Opinions about
these matters are as strongly held as they are varied. To date, however, there has been little systematic exploration of these questions,
and this must become a high-priority area for defense analysis in
coming years.

Foreign Sourcing

Considerable debate has also arisen over the wisdom of depending
on foreign suppliers for militarily relevant products. The United
States has a clear interest in spending limited defense budgets wisely,
in not squandering resources. In the absence of special considerations, buying from a high-cost domestic supplier when a lower-cost
foreign supplier is available cannot serve the national interest of
maintaining an effective military.

Special considerations will necessarily apply somewhat idiosyncrati-
cally to particular items. It is possible, however, to establish some
general guidelines for when domestic production should be prefered.

The United States should not, for example, depend on foreigners for products or designs the detailed workings and operational specifications of which need to be kept secret. (For example, the United States should not rely on foreign suppliers for acoustic gear used in antisubmarine operations.) Neither should it encourage, through it purchases, foreign production of the most sophisticated versions of operational equipment. The U.S. ability to control the flow of foreign-produced products is limited, and we will probably find that the higher costs of domestic production will be a small price to pay to make the proliferation of sophisticated weaponry less likely. (International coproduction arrangements for the new F-22 fighter, its radars, or its avionics suite, for example, are probably not wise.) The United States should not depend on foreign suppliers if a supply interruption could seriously degrade its ability to field or operate military forces.[20]

Although this last proposition may seem obvious, it probably provides little operational policy guidance today. The U.S. economy is very broad, and given enough time, it is undoubtedly capable of producing any product manufactured anywhere in the world. Thus, to oppose dependence on foreign suppliers, it is necessary also to argue that a supply interruption would have an important effect on military capabilities in the short run, before a new domestic source could be brought on line. Devising plausible scenarios that could result in such situations is not easy.

A more sophisticated version of this objection to reliance on foreign suppliers is the assertion that U.S. forces or U.S. defense contractors may not enjoy access to the very latest versions of foreign-produced components and may therefore find themselves a technological step behind the world standard. In civilian markets where the time be-

---

[20]The possibility that the supply of some militarily essential item may be interrupted is not, in itself, a sufficient reason to protect the operations of a high-priced U.S. producer. Continued purchases from a lower-priced foreign producer may be quite acceptable if it is possible to buy some form of "insurance" against a supply interruption. For some items, this insurance may take the form of stockpiling. In others, the insurance may be provided by opportunities to divert civilian production to military purposes in a time of crisis. For a fuller discussion, see Benjamin Zycher, Kenneth A. Solomon, and Loren Yager, *An "Adequate Insurance" Approach to Critical Dependencies of the Department of Defense*, Santa Monica, Calif.: RAND, R-3880-DARPA, 1991.

tween product generations is one or two years, a delay of a few months in getting access to the latest designs or components could be important. But the time between generations of military hardware is more often on the order of 10, 15, or even 20 years. Conventional wisdom also has it that components found in military systems are typically not as advanced as those found in civilian products sold in highly competitive civilian markets. In these circumstances, it is difficult to imagine that short-lived limitations on access to the very latest technology will be of much military significance.

For the routine supply of most military items, then, it seems unreasonable to insist on domestic production if foreign production will provide the needed goods more cheaply. As defense procurement spending shrinks in coming years and as the firms that make up the U.S. defense industrial base merge or go out of business, foreign suppliers of some defense goods may provide a welcome source of competition to the remaining U.S. suppliers and thereby save the Department of Defense (DoD) or upper-tier U.S. defense contractors from becoming overly dependent on domestic monopolists.

Rebuilding U.S. Military Forces

A defense industrial base that is able to do nothing more than meet the routine, noncrisis needs of the U.S. military, though, will not be adequate. Maintaining an effective military will also require maintaining the industrial capability to expand U.S. forces quickly, to replace lost equipment, or to replenish stocks of expendables. There is some evidence that modest efforts to encourage "smart" shutdown of current production lines—with tools and dies carefully stored and important know-how preserved (by, for example, videotaping the entire manufacture of the last production item)—can make possible much faster and less expensive reopening of these lines at some time in the future.[21] When surge demands must be met by production of new systems, it will be important to have designs for new systems "on the shelf," already tested at the prototype stage, and ready to go into production. From the beginning, these systems should be de-

[21]John Birkler, Joseph Large, Giles Smith, and Fred Timson, *Reconstituting a Production Capability: Past Experience, Restart Criteria, and Suggested Policies*, Santa Monica, Calif.: RAND, MR-273-ACQ, 1993.

signed to facilitate rapid production start-up, making use when possible of components, manufacturing equipment, and labor-force skills that can be drawn easily from civilian production.

Thus, any capability for rapidly expanded defense production requires a reservoir of components, equipment, and skilled labor in the civilian sector that can be drawn on for defense production if the need arises. One might imagine creating an industrial equivalent of the Civil Reserve Air Fleet (CRAF), through which the federal government provides modest subsidies to civilian industries to maintain certain equipment and labor-force skills likely to be of value if defense production had to be quickly increased. In return for the government subsidies, participating manufacturers would have to agree, for example, to maintain equipment in particular configurations (perhaps somewhat less than optimal for civilian use) or to give workers a small amount of time to maintain skills that may not be in current use and to agree to transfer this equipment and these workers to defense production when required by the government. Such programs, however, would presumably be practical for only a few easily specified types of equipment or work skills. For the most part, the reservoir from which resources for expanded military production will be drawn will be the general economy. Thus, the best guarantee that a surge in defense production will be possible will be provided by a productive, technologically sophisticated manufacturing sector staffed by skilled and flexible workers.

More caution may be required in relying on foreign suppliers for significantly expanded production than for routine procurement of military goods. A need for surge production may arise, one supposes, in times of international tension, and it is precisely at such times that foreign supply may be undependable. But even for surge purposes, foreign supply should not be ruled out entirely. The more firms or factories an item is bought from, the more opportunities there will be for increased production in a crisis. Spreading production of a key item to many suppliers—some of them perhaps foreign—may increase the surge capacity. Even domestic supply, after all, is not completely reliable. Immune, presumably, to politically motivated interruptions, domestic supplies are still vulnerable to technical, mechanical, or managerial failures. A network of potential suppliers, some of them foreign, may provide better insurance of supply in a crisis than a smaller network of purely domestic suppliers.

FOREIGN INVESTMENT IN THE UNITED STATES

Some concern has arisen in recent years over the actual or potential acquisition of U.S. assets—firms, financial instruments, buildings, farm land, even baseball teams—by foreigners.[22] At some visceral level, we harbor suspicions about consequences of such acquisitions. After all, when a foreigner outbids an American for some American asset, does not control of that asset pass from the former American owner to a new foreign owner? Does this not threaten our ability to "control our own economic destiny?"

For the most part, fears of foreign purchases of assets in the United States are unfounded. Fixed assets (factories, buildings, land, etc.) cannot, after all, be taken back to the new owner's native country. These assets remain in the United States providing jobs for U.S. workers and generating tax revenues for U.S. governments, just as if they were owned by U.S. citizens. Foreign owners operating assets in the United States are subject to all the laws of the United States. Foreign owners who violate these laws risk, ultimately, the loss of their assets. Indeed, it is not entirely clear who gains control over whom as a result of foreign purchases of fixed assets in the United States. To the extent that foreign investment in the United States results in the creation of new fixed assets, this investment may raise the productivity and the wages of U.S. workers and lead to higher total output in the U.S. economy.[23]

Laws governing the operation of business in the United States are not perfect, of course, and it is conceivable that a foreign owner of a U.S. factory or firm might operate that factory or firm in a manner

---

[22]For a thorough and insightful discussion of the issues of foreign investment in the United States, Edward M. Graham and Paul R. Krugman, *Foreign Direct Investment in the United States*, 2nd ed., Institute for International Economics, 1991.

[23]It is ironic, to say the least, that some of the same people who oppose foreign investment in the United States also complain about the "export of American jobs" that results from investments by American firms in other countries. You cannot have it both ways. If we lose something when a foreigner invests here, then logically we must gain something when Americans invest abroad.

that, although legal, we might find undesirable. A foreign-owned firm might, for example, reserve all senior management positions for citizens of the home country, thereby denying Americans the experience necessary to increase their job skills. A foreign-owned firm might transfer all R&D activities to the home country, thereby depriving the United States of some of the potential "spillover" benefits that may be generated by R&D activity. Foreign-owned firms might prefer to buy intermediate products and services from home-country suppliers, thereby reducing demand for U.S.-made substitutes. But a U.S. owner would also be free to engage in exactly these same practices. Anecdotes abound regarding alleged differences in behavior between U.S.-owned and foreign-owned firms in the United States, but to date there is no evidence of systematic differences in behavior. Research in this area is far from conclusive, but as far as we can tell today, there is no reason to believe that a Japanese foreman or a German landlord is any more difficult to deal with than his or her U.S. counterpart.

In a few industries where the United States attaches special importance to verifying the reliability, the judgment, or the *bona fides* of owners, it might reasonably resist acquisitions by foreigners. This is not because foreigners are believed to be less competent or more corrupt than U.S. resident, but simply because it may be much harder for U.S. authorities to investigate fully the background or past performance of someone whose previous activities have been conducted largely outside this country. This is why, for example, the U.S. government subjects would-be foreign purchasers of U.S. banks to special scrutiny and restrictions. Almost certainly, though, the government currently carries such restrictions too far. What danger does the United States run in allowing foreign ownership of U.S. air carriers[24] or of U.S. television stations?

The United States might also reasonably object to foreign acquisitions of some nonfixed and therefore transferable assets. Many

---

[24]Although restrictions on foreign ownership of U.S. air carriers had their origins in concerns about the dangers of foreign control of "strategic" transportation resources, these restrictions have been used in recent years as bargaining chips to gain improved access to foreign air transport markets by U.S. carriers. Whether or not these efforts will finally prove successful remains to be seen. However, increased opportunities for foreign ownership might promote increased competition in the U.S. market, to the benefit of U.S. consumers.

countries, for example, prohibit the sale to foreigners (or, more tech-nically, the removal from the country) of certain kinds of artistic trea-sures. The rationale here, of course, is that these treasures must be seen to be enjoyed, and their transfer abroad would deprive citizens in the source country of such enjoyment.

But what about other kinds of easily transferable assets? What about patents, know-how, and technical information? Here the question becomes more difficult. Is U.S. economic security enhanced by prohibiting the sale or transfer to foreigners of certain kinds of tech-nical information? If the information is of clear military value, its sale or transfer should almost certainly be restricted. But what about so-called dual-use technologies, which have both military and com-mercial applications? Perhaps the correct test to use in such cases is whether or not the U.S. government would feel comfortable in allow-ing the products made with the technology in question to be sold abroad unless, of course, the technology in question is already avail-able abroad. If the government fears the military consequences of allowing certain kinds of products to be sold abroad (advanced com-puters, say, or very sophisticated milling equipment), it should prob-ably prohibit the sale to foreigners of the company producing these products or the technological information on which this production depends.[25] With regard to purely commercial technologies, it is hard to see any justification for prohibiting sales or transfers to foreigners. If a U.S. owner believes that he or she can profit more by turning over certain patents or processes to foreigners than by retaining and exploiting those patents and processes, and if the local exploitation of the patents or processes in question generates no substantial local external benefit, no American can be expected to gain as a consequence of restrictions on sales or transfers.

Finally, there seems no reason to believe that the sale of U.S. finan-cial instruments to foreigners threatens U.S. national security in any appreciable way. Scenarios of financial turmoil that might be caused

---

[25]The (alleged) restrictiveness of U.S. export control laws is sometimes illustrated with the (usually untested) observation that it is sometimes easier to sell an entire company to a foreigner than it is to sell the products that company makes to the same foreigner. If this were true, something would be seriously amiss. If it is worth restricting the transfer of the product, it is worth restricting the transfer of the know-how that lies behind it.

by massive dumping of, say, U.S. treasury securities by foreign owners are better plot devices for movies and novels than they are realis-
tic possibilities. Anyone trying to engage in a massive dumping operation would almost certainly suffer severe losses in the process,
and it is therefore hard to imagine what motives would lie behind
such actions. More to the point, though, it is far from certain that an
attempt to sell large volumes of treasury securities would in fact
cause serious financial disruption. If someone is selling large volumes of securities, someone else is necessarily buying them. The
U.S. Treasury is largely indifferent about to whom it pays interest,
and the transfer of bonds from one owner to another would be of little significance. Financial markets do not clear instantly, of course,
and sudden, massive sales of securities might generate some volatile
price and interest-rate movements for a short period of time.
Monetary authorities in all the industrialized countries have means
to counter financial-market instability, however, and disruptions are
likely to be short lived. It is hard to contemplate any orchestrated
sell-off by foreign owners of U.S. securities that comes close in size to
the unorchestrated sell-off of securities that brought about the
October 1987 plunge in world stock markets. After a few days of
volatility, national and international financial markets returned to
normal operations, and the October crash had no lasting ill effects on
any national economy.

Chapter Four

A BROADER VIEW OF ECONOMIC SECURITY

Being bigger or richer than other countries is not, of course, a strategy for enhancing economic security that is open to most countries. We cannot all be bigger or richer than everybody else. Neither can all countries hope to be internationally dominant in a broad range of industries or industrial processes. Certainly, not all countries can aspire to being militarily dominant.

Even for the few large countries (for example, the United States or, within the European context, Germany) or groupings of countries (e.g., the EU) that might have a reasonable chance of gaining sufficient economic bulk to shape the world to their liking, a strategy of relying simply on size—whether relative or absolute—is no longer adequate. The United States was not sufficiently large or self-sufficient, for example, to be insulated from the consequences of reductions in oil output engineered by OPEC in the 1970s and 1980s. Neither has the United States in recent years been sufficiently dominant in international financial affairs to stabilize foreign exchange rates or to convince other countries to adopt policies that might lead to exchange-rate stability. Neither would the United States have been able unilaterally to prevent a contraction of world trade or to insulate itself from the consequences of such a contraction, had the recent round of multilateral trade negotiations unraveled. The United States is not and will probably never again be the world's leader in all advanced technologies and industrial processes.[1]

---

[1]Nor should we want to be. Natural endowments, local market conditions, history, and circumstances impart relative advantages to different countries in the development and exploitation of different technologies. Just as overall welfare is increased if

This state of affairs is not necessarily bad. U.S. inability to shape all aspects of the global economy or to dominate all aspects of global commerce is the result, at least in part, of U.S. integration into the world economy. This integration allows specialization. The United States no longer has to do everything for itself; for some things, it can rely on others. With this specialization comes increased efficiency and increased output for all concerned.

Seeking economic security simply through size, control, and relative economic performance is, in essence, seeking to avoid the negative consequences of external developments. If we are big and/or isolated from the world, most things that happen beyond our borders will not hurt us much. If we are dominant enough to shape the rules of the game, the desires and policies of other nations will not bother us very much. If our firms are securely dominant, we need not worry about commercial or industrial developments elsewhere.

An alternative approach (really a supplementary or complementary approach) is to seek to minimize the likelihood that negative external events will occur in the first place. In addition to doing what it can to limit its vulnerability to negative external developments, the United States should also seek ways to minimize international economic instability of the sort that may generate undesirable developments. The pursuit of international economic stability is closely analogous to and has much the same motivation as long-standing U.S. efforts to counter international political instability. As we will see in the remainder of this chapter, pursuing U.S. economic security will in many cases turn out to be the same thing as pursuing international economic stability.

MAINTAINING ACCESS TO FOREIGN MARKETS

The United States was created, in part, because residents of the American colonies bridled at trade restrictions imposed on them by the English government. Ever since, efforts to maintain and expand U.S. access to foreign markets—for purposes of both buying and

---

nations specialize in areas of production where they enjoy a comparative advantage, gains in overall welfare will likely result from international specialization in technological development.

selling—have constituted a central element of U.S. foreign and economic policy.

Integration of U.S. commercial and financial affairs with those of other countries unquestionably creates a certain susceptibility to shocks emanating elsewhere in the world. But by providing expanded markets for U.S. products, a wider range of choice for U.S. consumers, new opportunities for productive investments by Americans, and new sources of financing for private and public undertakings in the United States, this integration has also served to enhance the economic well-being of all U.S. residents. Today, much more so than in the 18th century, the economic well-being of U.S. residents depends on their ability to buy and to sell goods, services, and financial instruments in markets all over the world. And today, no less than in the 18th century, actions by foreign governments can and too frequently do restrict the freedom of U.S. resident to do so. Consequently, a major objective of U.S. economic security policy must be to protect and expand access by U.S. residents to foreign commercial and financial markets.

At the most basic level, U.S. economic security requires a reliable supply of the commodities and products necessary to support U.S. lifestyles and U.S. economic activity. Without doubt, the United States has the resources, the technological know-how, and the flexibility eventually to work around disruptions in the supply of nearly any commodity. Sudden supply interruptions of important commodities can nonetheless cause us considerable pain as, of course, the oil shocks of the 1970s and early 1980s illustrated. Decisions by Middle Eastern oil producers never threatened the political viability of the United States, of course. Nor did OPEC policies ever hold the potential for reducing U.S. GDP by any more than a few percentage points. Still, developments in international oil markets did cause inconvenience and lost production in the United States of a scale sufficient at least to tempt U.S. government officials to alter U.S. foreign and military policies. In this regard, U.S. sovereignty was to a degree compromised. Neither its economic nor its political security was absolute in the face of decisions by foreign oil producers.

The memory of the oil crises is fading today, but alarmists still call occasionally for U.S. government policies to decrease alleged U.S. "dependence" on foreign sources for this or that "essential" product or service. Frequently, the remedial policies proposed seek to increase the self-sufficiency of the United States in the production of the allegedly essential commodity.

But those who advocate policies of increased self-sufficiency have (except as noted above in the cases of some specialized military hardware) learned the wrong lesson from the oil crises of a decade and more ago. Self-sufficiency would not and should not have protected the United States from the consequences of sudden reductions in output by Middle East oil producers. Even if the United States had been completely self-sufficient in oil production, it would still have been wise to allow oil prices in the United States to rise along with world prices. To be sure, rapidly changing oil prices would have (in fact, did) cause considerable turmoil and impose considerable costs as factories, residences, transportation systems, etc., were restructured to reduce the use of suddenly more expensive oil. But to have ignored the high foreign price of oil, to have lived within U.S. self-sufficiency, refusing to sell U.S.-produced oil to the rest of the world, would have been to turn our backs on an opportunity to trade a U.S.-produced product for foreign-produced non-oil goods and services at suddenly much more advantageous terms of trade.

The pain caused by the oil shocks was caused by the rapid change in the relative price of an important commodity. The United States could have avoided this pain only by isolating itself from the larger world economy, a policy that would almost certainly have caused much greater pain. The aim of U.S. policy should not be self-sufficiency and the isolation that necessarily accompanies self-sufficiency, but rather a stable and dependable supply of important commodities, no matter where they are produced.

Oil was and remains today a special case among internationally traded commodities. No other commodity is as central to the functioning of modern industrialized economies and as difficult to find substitutes for in the short run. And the production of no other important commodity is as concentrated in politically unstable parts of the world. U.S. efforts to reduce tensions in the Middle East and to counter the rise of potentially destabilizing regional powers (Iraq, Iran) are important components of U.S. economic-security policy. U.S. economic security will be further enhanced by policies that help to reduce the concentration of production of important commodities in a few countries or a few regions of the world. U.S. aid to develop the oil export potential of Russia or Kazakhstan, for example, will reduce the concentration of world oil production in the Middle East and thereby increase U.S. and global economic security. Similarly, U.S. trade policies that allow imports of South Korean semiconductors will make it less likely that Japanese producers will achieve monopoly power in particular segments of this market. This kind of development will reduce concentration and enhance economic security.

Traditional thinking about economic security emphasized our access to market as buyers—whether or not we could depend on the supply of products we needed. More recently, attention seems to be shifting to the problems of market access as sellers—whether we will be able to sell our products in foreign markets. This is a legitimate concern. Buying and selling in international markets are, of course, intimately linked. Even if everyone is willing to sell to us, we cannot buy goods in international markets unless we are also able to sell there. We cannot indefinitely import more than we export. The prosperity and economic security of Americans depends just as much on our ability to sell as on our ability to buy.

But it is unlikely that U.S. producers can unilaterally enjoy access to foreign markets. U.S. access to foreign markets can be sustained in the long run only as part of a larger trading system that provides access for all producers to foreign markets. U.S. economic-security interests, then, will be served by promoting the worldwide expansion of international trade and investment and the elimination of barriers to such activities. International trade and investment are the basic building blocks of international economic relations, and the preservation of a stable international trading and investment environment is essential for preserving international economic stability. The experience of the 1930s provides a chilling illustration of the potential economic and political consequences of failure to maintain the international trading order.

Views differ sharply today on how best to promote international trade and to increase U.S. access to foreign markets:

- Through a renewed commitment to and possibly an extension of the principles of multilateralism and nondiscrimination (as exemplified in the GATT) or through the pursuit of bilateral or regional free-trading arrangements *à la* NAFTA?

- Through continued pursuit of the ideal of liberal (in the sense of free or market-determined) trade or through a more interventionist approach in which governments agree to influence trade patterns directly, attempting to overcome obstacles to trade that cannot be easily negotiated away?

- Through efforts to avoid or to defuse international disputes over trade matters or through more aggressively confrontational policies to force other nations to remove trade barriers?

There are respectable arguments on all sides of these issues, and the debates over appropriate trade policies will not be resolved any time soon. Certainly, they will not be resolved in this report. What is critical, however, is that international discussion and cooperation on trade matters continue, that some tangible progress toward expanding world trade continues to be made, and that trade be governed by understandable and predictable rules rather than by the whims of national governments.

Although they are apparently out of fashion in U.S. policy circles these days, patience and persistence in trade matters will also contribute to U.S. economic security. The frustrations generated by years of only glacial progress toward opening Japanese markets do not provide an adequate justification for abandoning efforts (inevitably slow and painful) to identify and to eliminate specific barriers to U.S. products. Resorting instead to demands for immediate adjustment of particular bilateral sectoral trade imbalances—by administrative means if necessary—risks locking in place patterns of trade that may be seen as beneficial today but cannot remain so indefinitely. If trade patterns are set today by government agreement rather than by market forces, what in the future will constitute an acceptable signal that these patterns should change?

For all of its size, diversity, and capacity for self-sufficiency, the United States is the world's largest trader, and consequently we have a major stake in preserving a smoothly functioning system of international trade. If the United States withdraws even a part of its support for market-determined trade, who else will step forward to preserve what may be the most important economic achievement of the postwar era?

A STABLE INTERNATIONAL FINANCIAL ENVIRONMENT

The modern financial environment is truly global. Capital flows almost perfectly freely these days among the world's major financial centers, and financial disturbances in any of these centers will be felt in all of the others. Stable and well-functioning U.S. financial markets will be possible only within a stable and well-functioning international financial environment. Thus, international financial stability will be a central objective of U.S. economic-security policy.

Exchange-Rate Management

It has been 20 years now since the final collapse of the system of fixed but adjustable exchange rates that was first outlined at the Bretton Woods conference of 1944. These years have been marked by dramatic swings in real exchange rates (exchange rates adjusted for differences in national price levels), which in turn have profoundly altered the international competitive prospects of firms all over the world. Entire industries and the jobs associated with them have been created in one country or lost in another as a consequence of exchange-rate movements. Workers have been displaced, and still-usable capital equipment has been idled. In the past 20 years, exchange-rate volatility and the sudden changes in national economic policies enacted (wisely or otherwise) to counter exchange-rate movements have constituted some of the most serious sources of uncertainty, and thus of economic insecurity, facing firms and individuals in the United States and throughout the world.

Volatile exchange rates are also seen by some as undermining support for market-driven trading regimes. If market forces that determine success or failure in international markets include the effects of widely swinging exchange rates, then some would prefer a more stable, even if somewhat less efficient, trading system in which trade patterns are protected by quantitative trade restrictions or negotiated among governments. But when governments rather than market forces determine the details of trade flows, routine commercial matters become political, and the potential for political confrontation over trade matters increases. Also, government efforts to counter the trade consequences of volatile exchange rates can have the effect of rigidifying world trade patterns, preventing necessary and desirable adjustments to changes in fundamental economic circumstances.

Finally, there is concern that fluctuating exchange rates may discourage certain types of investment. International investors may fear that their expected returns will evaporate as a consequence of an exchange-rate swing.[2] Domestic investors may shy away from sectors (manufacturing, for example) having a potential for foreign competition, preferring instead sectors (like some services) in which competition will be principally domestic and therefore not strongly influenced by unpredictable exchange-rate movements. Some have suggested that it is not a coincidence that growth rates of manufacturing productivity have declined worldwide since the collapse of the Bretton Woods exchange-rate system.

As with trade policy, there is considerable debate over the best methods for achieving increased exchange-rate stability. Some argue for direct efforts by governments to maintain fixed exchange rates. Others argue that fluctuating exchange rates are merely the symptoms of more fundamental failures by governments to pursue noninflationary economic policies and that wiser and steadier internal economic policies will bring exchange-rate stability as a by-product. There is little disagreement, however, that greater stability in real exchange rates than we have seen since the collapse of the Bretton Woods system would contribute both to overall prosperity (through increased trade and investment) and to international economic security (by reducing the likelihood of painful shocks).

---

[2]Many investment projects (building, say, a new factory) require years to complete. Unfortunately, forward foreign markets do not typically offer opportunities to hedge against exchange-rate movements more than about a year in the future. While forward currency contracts of longer maturities are written from time to time, the market for long-maturity futures is very thin. For practical purposes, investors cannot usually buy protection against the consequences of an adverse exchange-rate movement a few years in the future.

International Capital Flows and Economic Policy Coordination

Closely related to exchange-rate instability are large and unpredictable international capital movements. It is now possible (and routine) for portfolio managers to move tens of millions of dollars (or the equivalent in yen, deutsche marks, pounds, or francs) electronically across national boundaries or from one currency to another in a matter of minutes. So easy has it become to move very large sums that even the slightest hint that exchange rates may change triggers massive flows, which help to precipitate precisely the changes that were anticipated. In this sense, ever-improving facilities for managing large financial transactions have contributed to exchange-rate volatility. As repeated currency crises—most recently the European currency crises of September 1992 and August 1993—have illustrated, national monetary authorities are sometimes powerless to counter the effects of very large private capital flows.

Schemes for slowing down international capital movements are proposed from time to time. (The most common proposals usually involve some sort of transaction tax designed to "throw sand into the works" of international capital movements.) There is little support today, though, for efforts to control capital mobility. The rapid proliferation of new financial instruments in recent years has made it ever easier for portfolio managers to avoid specific national measures aimed at limiting international capital mobility; every new class of financial instruments creates a potential hole for would-be controllers of capital flows to plug. Most governments have recognized the impossibility of the task of effectively controlling international capital movements, and the thrust of most recent policy initiatives has, in fact, been in just the opposite direction—toward liberalization of financial markets.

In today's international financial environment, large flows of "hot money" and the problems they cause will be avoided only if national economic policies are sufficiently stable and consistent with each other so as not to create incentives for large cross-border or cross-currency flows in the first place. Thus, policymakers must choose the kind of economic security they want to pursue. On the one hand, they may seek to preserve their ability to set national economic policies independently of policies in other countries by insulating themselves from foreign economic and financial developments abroad. This provides a sort of economic security in the sense that insulation from international financial markets, if successful, preserves a nation's ability to control its own economic and financial destiny.

Alternatively, national policymakers can seek increased economic stability—and with it increased economic security—by giving up a degree of policy autonomy and making macroeconomic policy jointly with other nations.

There is considerable debate over the most effective operational strategies for pursuing international coordination of national economic policies, over the rigor with which international policy consistency should be pursued and over the wisdom in particular circumstances of sacrificing one macroeconomic goal (say, low inflation) for another (say, exchange-rate stability). Plausible approaches range from the very loose and informal consultative processes by which the G-7 industrialized countries try to manage their affairs, through efforts at explicit exchange-rate targeting, to the establishment of "convergence criteria" for national inflation rates or public deficits, all the way to full economic and monetary union, as proposed for the EU. Despite the debate over appropriate approaches to policy coordination, there is today a growing recognition that, as financial markets become more integrated, the former sort of economic security, based on isolation, becomes less and less practical. Increasingly, there is no practical choice but to pursue economic security through some sort of international policy cooperation.[3]

PROMOTING MARKET-ORIENTED ECONOMIC POLICIES

For a variety of reasons, the United States has an interest in promoting market-oriented economic policies in other countries. Both theory and experience suggest that market-oriented policies, with

---

[3]Ironically, even efforts to insulate a national economy from international financial instability would probably require careful international coordination, at least at the outset. A single nation suspected of contemplating a tax or other form of limitation on capital movements would experience massive capital flight as portfolio managers sought to put their assets beyond its reach. This kind of turbulence could be avoided only if a large group of nations were able to impose similar restrictions simultaneously.

minimal state involvement in production and distribution decisions, provide the most promising paths to economic growth.[4] Material prosperity is certainly not the only requirement for political stability, but in most cases it helps. Thus, promoting market-oriented economic policies abroad indirectly advances U.S. interests in international political stability. Also, market-oriented economic systems are typically pluralistic, with economic decisionmaking and the power to shape economic events distributed among many players, rather than concentrated in the hands of the government. To the extent that economic power offers access to political power, market-oriented systems may therefore advance U.S. interests in promoting pluralistic government abroad.

Finally, the advancement of market-oriented policies abroad may yield direct economic benefits for the United States. Market mechanisms and market forces dominate the functioning of the U.S. economy. The unfettered action of market forces will not necessarily produce the most desirable outcomes, however, when the market-driven U.S. economy interacts with government-managed foreign economies. As advocates of more aggressively interventionist policies repeatedly (and sometimes correctly) point out, U.S. reliance on market forces is not always the best course in the face of highly interventionist actions (subsidies, trade restrictions, etc.) by other countries.[5] But for practical as well as philosophical reasons, the United States is unlikely to change its own free-market orientation. If other countries are encouraged to adopt similar policies, the likelihood that U.S. free-market policies will turn out to be optimal is increased.

---

[4]This is not to say that all state intervention is necessarily counterproductive. The examples of Japan, South Korea, and Singapore come immediately to mind. Even in these countries, though, the state role was and is restricted to selected sectors in economies driven primarily by market forces, and the state role has decreased over time. It is hard to think of any country where economic performance has been enhanced by increasing the state role, and there are numerous examples of the opposite phenomenon.

[5]Whatever may be the shortcomings of market forces in particular circumstances, it is wise to bear in mind the all-too-frequent shortcomings of nonmarket alternatives. Government efforts to supersede or to improve upon market mechanisms can fall prey to bureaucratic ineptitude, maneuvering by special interest groups, and (occasionally) outright corruption. We should be wary of replacing a market failure with a "nonmarket failure."

One key to promoting the rise of market-oriented economic policies abroad will be making sure that countries pursuing such policies as part of development or economic-reform efforts enjoy access to dependable sources of international credit and capital. Ideally, development and reform efforts will be financed through private international credit markets—through lending by private international banks and through private foreign direct investment. International financial markets have expanded greatly in the last 20 years and now, in fact, do provide the bulk of the financing available to developing and reforming economies.

But private credit and capital markets will probably never become fully satisfactory or adequate channels for development and reform financing. In the past, for example, commercial banks have shown a tendency toward inconsistent and herd-like behavior with regard to development lending, all granting or withholding credit at the same time. In the late 1970s, for example, banks were quite eager to lend to developing countries, encouraging (in the eyes of some) considerable overborrowing. The "debt crisis" of the early 1980s, of course, brought a sharp reversal of attitudes, and even well-managed and perfectly creditworthy countries encountered difficulty in attracting necessary financing. Some other source of international credit—more dependably available than credit from private banks, less likely to be withdrawn at the first indications of trouble in a borrowing country—may be required. Similarly, foreign direct investors are unlikely ever to show much interest in social infrastructure projects like road-building, development of water systems, establishment of schools or hospitals, etc. Some other source of financing may be required for such projects.

Today, these gaps in international credit and capital markets are at least partially filled by official multilateral credit-granting institutions, such as the World Bank, the International Monetary Fund, and the various regional development banks. As a practical matter, supporting development and reform efforts will require continued support for these institutions, at least for the foreseeable future. Credit from official sources has not always produced the anticipated or hoped-for positive results. Arguably, such credit has in some cases served only to prop up inefficient economic systems or to perpetuate unsound policies in borrowing countries, actually delaying needed reforms. Existing multilateral credit institutions are far from perfect, and efforts to improve these institutions and their policies are still required.[6] It may even be necessary to create new multilateral channels for development and reform finance.[7]

MAINTAINING A FUNCTIONING INTERNATIONAL COMMERCIAL AND FINANCIAL INFRASTRUCTURE

Modern commercial and financial life is complex. Routine activity depends on an extensive array of facilitating services: transportation, information, brokering, payment, credit, leasing, etc. Also necessary are commonly accepted rules and procedures for carrying out transactions. These rules and procedures cover such matters as dispute settlement, contract enforcement, and settlement of accounts payable. When these services are lacking or when the rules of the game break down, commerce is hindered. The economic well-being of U.S. residents depends on the smooth conduct of national and international commerce, and hence on the smooth and efficient functioning of what we might think of as a commercial and financial infrastructure. Preserving U.S. economic security requires protecting this infrastructure from accidental or intentional disruption.

Traditionally, the most basic elements of the international commercial infrastructure have been the freedom of peaceful international passage for trade purposes and the sanctity of property rights. Throughout its history, the United States has exercised its diplomatic

---

[6]High on the list of needed reforms would be a more careful delineation of the increasingly overlapping responsibilities of the IMF and the development banks. We might also seek, for example, increased lending to private enterprises rather than to governments in developing or reforming countries, more aggressive promotion of privatization programs, greater attention to the environmental consequences of development programs, or greater efforts to make sure that the benefits of economic growth and development are broadly shared within the borrowing country. Above all, there is a need for critical review of the effects of lending by the IMF and the multilateral development banks and of the policies they encourage borrowing countries to adopt. No one has a clear recipe for successful economic development or reform, and mistakes will inevitably be made. At the very least, we should learn from these mistakes.

[7]The difficulties that the Western industrialized democracies have encountered in trying to devise a unified approach to providing economic assistance to the former Soviet Union, for example, suggest that the existing multilateral institutions are not entirely adequate for such an important task. A workable framework for coordinated international assistance has yet to be devised.

and military muscle to protect U.S. access to international shipping routes. Similarly, the U.S. government has sought to protect U.S.-owned foreign assets from confiscation or expropriation. These and their modern-day variants (e.g., the right of peaceful overflight) will continue to be important objectives of U.S. economic security policy.

In recent years, we have come to recognize the importance of other elements of this infrastructure. Moreover, we have come to recognize that some of these additional elements are vulnerable to disruption and are therefore appropriate objectives for policies aimed at enhancing U.S. and international economic security.

Of particular concern in this regard is the international banking system. In today's world, commercial banks play an essential role in international trade and investment. They facilitate international payments, provide short-term trade financing and related trade documentation services, guarantee payment among parties who do not have recourse to common legal systems, channel funds from countries with savings surpluses to countries with savings deficits, and generally provide the lubrication necessary to keep the wheels of international commerce turning. If the international banking system is weakened or if parties to transactions begin to doubt the reliability of international banks, the volume of international credit and other financial services will be restricted, generally to the detriment of international trade and investment. More catastrophically, a failure of one bank can render the claims of other banks uncollectable, possibly causing these other banks to default on their obligations, and so on. If the original defaults are of sufficient size, the result can be a sudden and widespread contraction of credit and banking services. For these reasons, the stability of the international banking system and the soundness of individual banks doing international business have come increasingly to be seen as "international public goods" in which all nations have an interest, which no nation can obtain solely through its own efforts, and for which therefore all nations bear a degree of responsibility.

Recent years have seen some progress toward strengthening the international banking system. International agreements have been concluded delineating, for example, the responsibilities of national authorities in regulating the activities of international banks, clarifying which central banks bear responsibility for serving as "lenders of last resort" for banks facing liquidity difficulties, and establishing international standards for bank capital adequacy. These agreements mark significant steps forward in removing potential sources of international economic uncertainty and instability. Much remains to be accomplished in this regard, however. The recent collapse of the Bank of Credit and Commerce International (BCCI) is a reminder that oversight arrangements for banks operating in multiple countries are still something less than satisfactory. Also, the international community is still struggling to establish capital adequacy standards for securities firms undertaking international business.

A more recent concern has been the potential vulnerability of electronic clearing arrangements (the so-called financial wires) through which banks settle accounts with each other. The volume of funds routinely moving over the financial wires is staggering. The flow of funds through the Clearing House Interbank Payments System (CHIPS), the principal system for international interbank transfers, is estimated at the equivalent of $1 trillion *per day*. Because of timing differences in when funds are debited and credited, operations of the financial wires produce enormous volumes of very short-term, intra-day credit. Failure of a clearing system, whether a result of computer malfunction or malicious action, could have severe financial repercussions: Funds expected by banks would not arrive, making it impossible for these banks to meet their obligations to other banks, and so on down the line. Responsibilities for regulating international financial wires and for intervening in the event of trouble are not well spelled out today.

Some troubling gaps have also become apparent in the structure of international agreements regulating international trade and investment. International protection of intellectual property rights, for example, is far from adequate today, and U.S. residents—because they create a large share of the world's intellectual property—are among the principal victims of this inadequacy. The absence of an effective enforcement mechanism for international trade agreements causes difficulties for many countries and has led to some dangerous confrontations over trade matters. In 1992, for example, after five years of fruitless efforts to convince the European Community to comply with international rulings regarding agricultural subsidies, the United States saw no alternative but to threaten strenuous retaliatory action unless the EU changed its policies. In the event, the EU did back down, but only after exposing the United States, Europe, and perhaps the rest of the world to the possibility of a ruinous trade war. A third gap in the international rules of the game is the absence of effective international competition policy—extensions of national anti-trust laws to prohibit the cartelization of international markets by combinations of firms from several countries. The EU is working its way toward a Union-wide competition policy, but as yet no similar effort has been launched toward the rest of the world.

EQUITABLE INCOME DISTRIBUTION

True national security—of the military or the economic variety—requires a unified populace with a common understanding of national interests and capable of standing together in the face of foreign challenges. Essential to this kind of national unity is a shared perception that "we are all in this together," that all citizens are being treated fairly, and that no part of the population is granted special favors or called upon to make special sacrifices. In the economic sphere, this translates into a requirement to maintain a distribution of income and economic well-being that is perceived to be broadly fair and that does not exclude large portions of the population from the general prosperity.

There has been much discussion in the last two or three years of the apparently widening gap between the top and the bottom of the U.S. income distribution. Although there is disagreement over the full set of factors that may have contributed to this widening, there is a general recognition that the increasing openness of the U.S. economy has complicated the task of maintaining the incomes of the poorest and least skilled U.S. residents.

Most Americans have benefited from the fuller integration of the U.S. economy into the larger world economy. New markets have been opened for U.S. products, and U.S. consumers now enjoy a wider choice of goods available for purchase. But lower-skilled U.S. workers increasingly find themselves in competition with the enormous pool of low-skilled and low-paid labor in the rest of the world. The results are lower wages for low-skilled U.S. workers. When wages can go no lower because of minimum-wage laws, low-skilled workers simply lose jobs. A continuing flow of low-skilled immigrants compounds the problem.

The ideal response to growing competition for low-skilled jobs in the United States is to improve the skill levels of U.S. workers, so that they will no longer have to compete with low-paid foreign workers. This is, of course, much more easily said than done. Theories about how to train better workers abound, but few programs have shown clearly successful results in practice. In even the most optimistic scenarios, years will be required to bring about significant improvements in the skills of the least-educated U.S. residents. A second-best approach would be to provide tax relief or income supplements for the working poor and enhanced benefits for the unemployed, to maintain their incomes at what are perceived to be acceptable levels for U.S. citizens. But proposals for such income transfers create what many consider undesirable incentives and often face stiff political opposition.[8]

When efforts to raise skill levels or to supplement the incomes of low-skilled workers are unfeasible or ineffective, governments face pressures to protect low-skilled workers from the consequences of international competition by limiting imports of foreign goods. (Concern over wages and employment opportunities for low-skilled U.S. workers generated serious opposition to a free-trade agreement with Mexico.) While protectionist policies may indeed improve the lot of some of the poorest U.S. workers, they will almost certainly reduce the overall level of prosperity in the United States, by driving up the prices that all consumers must pay for affected products and by inviting protectionist policies in other countries. As difficult as other approaches may be, trade restrictions cannot be an appropriate tool for maintaining an equitable income distribution and social harmony.

Some progress toward raising the incomes of the least skilled might be achieved by trying to promote increased productivity in industries that employ low-skilled workers. Doing so, though, would require a reversal of current conventional wisdom about what sorts of industries should receive special assistance or encouragement from the government. Emerging high-technology industries are the most frequently suggested targets for special government assistance, and,

---

[8]But not always. Changes in U.S. tax law enacted in 1993 increased the earned income tax credit.

as we have already noted, there are plausible arguments in favor of support for some of these industries. But there may also be good social reasons for focusing public policy on a very different set of industries: those that provide employment for lower-skilled and less-well-educated workers. Public resources devoted to improving production efficiency in U.S. high-technology industries might conceivably be better spent in efforts to improve the productivity (R&D, perhaps, or subsidies for capital investment) and thus the wages of lower-skilled workers in other, relatively "low-tech," industries.

Generally, professionals and highly skilled production workers in the United States do not have a difficult time finding employment. Recessions and structural changes in the economy (like the current reductions in defense production) do, of course, displace highly trained workers from time to time; but unemployment rates for well-educated workers generally remain low.[9] Consequently, there is probably not a lot of social gain in creating increased employment opportunities for the highly skilled. Because such workers usually require extensive education or training, the supply of skilled workers cannot be expanded quickly to meet increased demand. Promoting growth in industries that make heavy use of skilled workers may do nothing but bid up the wages of the limited supply of skilled workers available.

The circumstances of less-skilled workers may be very different. There seems to be a more or less constant reservoir of unemployed low-skilled workers in the United States. Continuing immigration may add to this oversupply. Unemployment rates for poorly educated workers are high, and these high levels of unemployment can give rise to a variety of social ills that impose costs on all parts of society. It may be that social cohesion and the longer-run economic

---

[9]A Department of Labor study found the following unemployment rates for workers with varying levels of educational achievement in 1987:

Less than four years of high school	11.1%
4 years of high school	6.3%
1 to 3 years of college	4.5%
4 years of college or more	2.3%

See Wayne J. Howe, "Education and Demographics: How Do They Affect Unemployment Rates?" *Monthly Labor Review*, January 1988, pp. 3–12.

security of the United States are better served by government programs that aim to promote industries that will provide jobs for less-skilled workers and to promote technical innovation that will increase the productivity—and thus the wages—of lower-skilled workers. Rather than seeking better ways to make semiconductors or advanced airframes, perhaps public resources should be directed to revitalizing, say, the U.S. textile, garment, or food-processing industries or other industries that are commonly thought of as "low-tech."

Chapter Five

ECONOMIC POWER

ECONOMIC SECURITY, ECONOMIC POLICY, AND SECURITY POLICY

Economic security can be viewed through two different lenses: one focuses on the national security dimensions of economic policy, the other on the economic dimensions of national security policy. The first lens concentrates on the national security effects and consequences of economic measures and economic policies. This includes consideration of how the economy's performance affects the international security position of the United States. Most of the discussion in the preceding chapters has viewed economic security through this lens. Thus, its scope has encompassed the security reasons for seeking to limit the uncertainty and instability of U.S. economic growth while raising its magnitude; the security reasons why it may be germane that the U.S. economy should be "number 1" in the world economy; the case for having large, competitively and technologically vigorous firms; the special importance that may be attributed to certain key sectors and technologies; and the security benefits associated with a robust and stable global economic and financial infrastructure. We have dwelt at some length, in the preceding discussion, with these security dimensions of economic policies because of their prominence in the public debate, as well as the frequent looseness if not obscurity accorded these matters in the media.

Organizationally, within the U.S. policy community, responsibility for the security dimensions of economic policy is spread across a large number of agencies that have principal jurisdiction over the numerous instruments and measures of economic policy. These agencies include the Department of the Treasury, the Department of Commerce, the Department of State, the U.S. Trade Representative, the International Trade Commission, and the National Economic Council. The DoD is an occasional, but usually only a secondary, player in this arena.

The second lens provides a different view of "economic security." This view encompasses the economic dimensions of national security policy, focusing on the economic effects and consequences of national security policies. Defense and military policy are more directly and conspicuously involved, and the roles of the DoD, the National Security Council, and the intelligence community are of central importance. From this perspective, "economic security," construed as the economic dimensions of national security policy, has two components. The first deals with ways in which military instruments may be used to generate economic effects; the second is concerned with ways in which economic instruments may be used to generate military effects by substituting for, supplementing, or reinforcing military ones in strengthening U.S. defense policy.

We address both components in the following discussion. Although the discussion is briefer than the previous treatment of the security dimensions of economic policies, we regard the economic dimensions of security policies as of equal importance. And, as noted above, the economic dimensions of security policies are and should be of particular concern to the DoD.

USING DEFENSE RESOURCES FOR ECONOMIC PURPOSES

The first component focuses on how economic considerations and criteria can affect the management, use, and allocation of resources earmarked for defense purposes. To illustrate how military instruments and resources may be used for their economic effect, we touch briefly on dual-use technology, the use of military capabilities to advance nondefense objectives, international burden-sharing, arms exports, and economic intelligence.

Dual-Use Technology

In some instances—perhaps more in the future than in the past—a choice among alternative military R&D projects, or among alternative ARPA-supported technologies, may be influenced by anticipated or hoped-for economic side effects. A case in point is the development of composite materials connected with the stealth program and the consideration of whether and how these composites may result in benefits for the private sector. Of course, a standard part of the debate over "industrial policy" between the United States, on the one hand, and Japan and Europe, on the other, has been the latter's argument that U.S. defense R&D has in fact functioned as a powerful source of defense subsidy for commercially lucrative spin-offs (e.g., the development of wide-body jet aircraft), thereby justifying compensatory subsidization by European and Japanese governments of their favored technologies and industries. However, there is a flaw in this argument. The commercially valuable side effects of U.S. military R&D in the past resulted (inadvertently) from efforts whose principal and explicit aim was to contribute to producing an international "public" good—namely, increased (NATO) military capabilities in the West's struggle with the Soviet Union—from which Europe and Japan benefited along with the United States. No corresponding public good from which the United States would benefit results from European and Japanese industrial policies.

A central question that arises in considering the meaning of "economic security" in the future is whether dual-use benefits should become an explicit and deliberate aim of U.S. security policy and of the use of defense resources. The argument for an affirmative answer is that there may well be instances in which a marginal modification or adjustment in the technologies and R&D programs that the DoD supports may also generate commercial payoffs and, hence, that these spin-off benefits should be made an explicit part of the decisionmaking process governing the use of defense R&D resources. The counterargument is that such spin-off benefits would not be sufficient to offset the suboptimal military R&D that would be undertaken in the quest for these benefits. To the extent that U.S. policymakers impute greater value to the spin-offs, and evince less concern for the military payoffs that may be forgone, they are likely to push dual-use technology in favor of this trade-off.

Joint-Use of Military Capabilities

A second example of the dual-use of military resources is the employment of military forces, airlift, logistics, engineering, and medical services to provide emergency assistance and relief in economic development and nation-building in support of U.S. policies in other countries. The experience of "Operation Provide Hope" in 1991 in Russia and Ukraine and the other republics of the former Soviet Union is a case in point. Indeed, the argument can be made that selected use of such capabilities may even serve certain military training and operational purposes at very low marginal costs in relation to the economic benefits thereby produced.[1] Economically beneficial results may thus be more efficiently obtained by using defense capabilities than by trying to obtain them in other ways.

International Burden-Sharing

It seems evident that, notwithstanding the U.S. position as the sole global superpower, the structure and pattern of international peacemaking and peacekeeping in the emergent world order will more often be collective and multilateral and will involve the United Nations or other collective bodies to a much greater extent than in the past. This evolving pattern entails both the sharing of responsibility, on the one hand, and of burdens and costs on the other. How these burdens are determined, and the forms in which they are to be shared (whether, for example, in hard currency, in manpower, or through the contribution of other resources) remains to be determined. It is not clear, for instance, whether the United Nations contribution formula is appropriate or whether adjustments should be made that allow for differing regional interests or for contributions in kind. Moreover, these economic dimensions of collective security arrangements, and how they are adjudicated, are likely to have profound effects on the political and military efficacy of the evolving United Nations or other collective security structures. To the extent that U.S. security policy encompasses collective security undertak-

---

[1]See Steedman Hinckley's RAND report on *Department of Defense Assistance to the Former Soviet Republics: Potential Applications of Existing Army Capabilities*, MR-245-A, relating to the use of Army capabilities for nation-building purposes. (RAND Graduate School doctoral dissertation, 1993.)

ings, sharing the burdens of such undertakings becomes part of the economic agenda of security policy.

Arms Exports

In the post–Cold War era, when defense procurement budgets in the United States and almost all major industrial countries are declining, incentives to increase exports of advanced conventional weapons are becoming stronger. Such exports become especially appealing both to U.S. and foreign defense firms to spread fixed tooling and over-head costs over a larger production base. These arms exports can also help maintain a critical minimum of design and technological expertise necessary to sustain the progress of military technology.

Two additional arguments can be adduced in favor of arms exports: First, arms exports to such key friends and allies of the United States as South Korea, Turkey, Israel, Egypt, Taiwan, Saudi Arabia, and Pakistan may strengthen regional deterrence and reduce the risk of aggression against them. Second, forgoing U.S. arms exports would simply result in increased sales by one or more of the other principal weapons exporters—Russia, France, China, or Britain.

As a result of these considerations, as well as the high quality of U.S. weapon technology, the U.S. share of the global arms market has in-creased substantially to more than half of the $50 billion annual global market, compared with approximately 25 percent in the 1980s. Arms exports carry with them serious, but often neglected, down-stream risks. The collective security structures referred to earlier may be more severely stressed by the proliferation of advanced mili-tary technology in various turbulent regions of the world and by the higher levels of violence that may ensue in conflicts in these regions. One corollary of this dilemma is to seek some form of stabilization and control to moderate weapons exports, rather than unrealistically attempting to eliminate it.[2] Another corollary is to include among the objectives of security policy the development of new technology and systems that can serve as promising countermeasures to offset the increased capabilities that are being acquired in potentially un-stable regions of the world as a result of exports of advanced

---

[2]See the discussion of "Arms Trade and Arms Control" below.

weapons, e.g., improving Patriot interceptors to counter improved Scud missiles.

Economic and Security Intelligence

One of the potentially important economic dimensions of security policy arises from the intensified competition among firms and countries in the world economy. In this competitive environment, the temptation for individual firms—some of which are partly or substantially owned by foreign governments—to engage in industrial espionage, perhaps with the assistance of their national governments, may grow. The aim is to get a leg up on the competition by acquiring the benefits of the competition's proprietary research without paying its costs. In trying to ascertain the extent to which such practices have occurred, are continuing, and may increase, the U.S. intelligence community may have a more active, as well as countervailing, role to play in the future.

USING ECONOMIC RESOURCES FOR DEFENSE PURPOSES

The second component of the economic dimensions of national security policy focuses on the role and use of economic instruments to advance the purposes of national security policy. These economic instruments can be defined and exercised separately from military and diplomatic instruments in their ability to protect or advance U.S. national interests. However, the effectiveness of economic instruments can often be significantly enhanced by conjoining their use with that of the other instruments.

As elements of national security policy, economic instruments can influence the behavior of other countries by conferring economic benefits or imposing economic costs or by displaying a credible capacity to do so. Foreign economic aid, as well as military aid, technical assistance, and most-favored nation status, can be used to confer such benefits. Economic sanctions, embargoes, freezing of financial assets, restricting access to the U.S. market, or heavily taxing such access can be used to impose economic costs.

When economic instruments are used as adjuncts of security policy, they can be compared to military instruments and can be evaluated in relation to the latter's capacity to affect behavior. Military instruments provide a means of influencing behavior in the international arena by deterrence or compellence, that is, by using force (rather than imposing economic costs), or credibly threatening to use it, to dissuade other countries from using it, or by using force to coerce, preempt, or repel their attempts to use it.

Besides their possible use as substitutes for the use of force, economic instruments can be used—whether as "carrots" or "sticks"—to enhance the effectiveness of military instruments in the pursuit of security objectives. For example, financial assets may be frozen instead of, or in addition to, the enforcement of a naval blockade.

Measuring Economic Instruments

Several economic indicators or metrics can be used to define and size the nation's capacity to generate economic instruments that bear directly or indirectly on security policy. These include gross national or domestic product (GNP or GDP), population (and hence, labor supply and per capita GNP), and a country's current account surplus. GNP and per capita GNP are typically used in discussions of economic power or of changes that occur in the *relative* economic power of countries. Inclusion of the current account surplus as an economic instrument is based on the questionable premise that it represents a current capital resource that, in principle at least, can be guided or shunted by using one policy device or another toward or away from a particular target country that may be the object of a nation's power. However, there are serious constraints on such uses because of the typically decentralized processes that determine international capital flows. Consequently, the ability of government policy to exercise a controlling influence on the amounts and directions of capital flows is usually limited.

At a more disaggregative level, the economic instruments of power can be defined in terms of particular components or sectors of the economy that are believed to have special significance, for example, advanced and advancing technology sectors, such as telecommunications, microelectronics, semiconductors, fiber optics, and bioengineering. The special significance attached to these key sectors resides in the economywide, growth-promoting effects they may generate; or in the monopoly market power (and hence supernormal profits) that may result from them; or in their anticipated connection to present or future military capabilities, including capabilities to protect and defend against the military capabilities of others. Similarly, specific components of the population and the general labor pool may be considered of greater significance as economic instruments of power than the population as a whole, for example, certain particular types of skilled labor; scientists; engineers; managers; design, production, and marketing experts; and computer scientists.

Apart from the current account surplus, another component of a country's international accounts can provide a type of economic power, for example, the size of its market to which foreign access may be permitted or denied, which can be roughly approximated by its level of imports. Thus, a country's level of *imports* is potentially a source of economic power, as well as its exports. Also, within the total international accounts, the nation's exports of goods and services constitute instruments of economic power that can be directed toward or away from foreign areas. Restricting access to U.S. goods' markets, or threatening to do so has, in fact, been more frequently used as a policy instrument than restricting access to U.S. capital markets.

As measures of economic power, these indicators have some utility, as well as serious flaws, especially so for the more aggregative measures. For example, one flaw arises from the fact that the measures may be inconsistent with one another and may move in opposite directions. Thus, on the one hand, the U.S. GNP as a share of the global product, has remained remarkably constant over the last 20 years (about 23 percent), and indeed has probably increased in the last 2 years due to stagnant or negative growth in Japan, Germany, and the former Soviet Union.[3] On the other hand, the U.S. current account has remained in deficit over the past decade, thereby weak-

---

[3]According to certain premises of economic theory—specifically, concave welfare functions and the diminishing marginal utility of income—the imposition of costs, or the threat of imposing them, may be a more effective means of influencing the behavior of particular countries than conferring benefits. The point may be particularly valid for countries that have relatively higher income levels, while the converse—benefits (carrots) more effective than cost imposition (sticks)—may be more effective if applied to countries with lower income levels.

ening the ability of U.S. policymakers to direct net capital resources toward or away from particular target areas.

Another reason such aggregate measures are seriously flawed as indicators of effective economic power is that the resources they measure are not credibly disposable or mobilizable for direct application to specific purposes in specific foreign areas. Limitations on the availability or disposability of aggregate resources arise from different sources. For example, China's GNP is currently perhaps two-thirds that of Japan in purchasing power parity terms, and India's GNP is perhaps one-fifth that of Japan. Yet both China and India are constrained in their ability to mobilize these large resources because of the enormous consumption demands of their respectively large populations.[4]

A different, but no less binding, constraint affects the U.S. capacity to mobilize its aggregate resources for foreign-policy purposes. This constraint arises from decentralization of economic decisionmaking in a market-based economy, thereby limiting the ability of government to direct, for foreign-policy purposes, the use and application of resources that are privately owned and produced.

The indicators of economic instruments of security policy can be compared to indicators of the military instruments of security policy. These, at an aggregative level, include total military spending, the size and quality of military forces, and the magnitude and quality of the military capital stock. And, at a more disaggregative level, the military instruments entail specific types of forces and capabilities: airlift and sealift projection forces, delivery systems, command and control and intelligence capabilities, and so on.

Although it is quite clear that the economic instruments we have referred to encounter major limitations in the effectiveness with which they can be used as adjuncts of security policy, it should not be forgotten that the military instruments themselves are often of limited effectiveness in their ability to protect and advance national objectives. Military instruments were not sufficient to win in Vietnam, and

---

[4]See Charles Wolf, Jr., Gregory Hildebrandt, Michael Kennedy, et al., *Long-Term Economic and Military Trends, 1950–2010*, RAND, N-2757-USDP, April 1989, Santa Monica, Ca.

the effectiveness of their past or prospective use in such differing situations as Northern Ireland and Bosnia is subject to limitations and constraints that are no less formidable than those that attend to the use of economic instruments to further U.S. security policy.

Key Industries and Technologies

The argument about nurturing key industries and technologies as elements of security policy relates in part to their presumed criticality in the exercise of *leverage* in the international arena. Such leverage, it is suggested, can be exercised by the United States if these industries and technologies are vigorous and productive within the U.S. economy, but leverage may be exercised against the United States if they are not. In the latter instance, the United States becomes dependent on the corresponding industries and technologies in other countries.

The reasoning in this instance is that these sectors and technologies are believed to have special attributes and importance because of the potential military applications they entail, or because of the dependency in which they place the economies of other countries or the invulnerability they enable the U.S. economy to achieve from possible coercion by others.

On one side of this argument are those who contend that only the overall size of an economy is important in determining the economic leverage it can exercise over other countries and that the specific composition of its industry is less relevant for this purpose. They argue that military power and mobilization capability are related to the overall size of the economy and that other forms of leverage (such as those discussed above) are also related to the size of the economy.

On the other side of the argument is the contention that computer chips really do matter more than potato chips, as the saying goes, or that a boom in residential construction will benefit the U.S. economy and its consumers, but is unlikely to confer any particular leverage over the behavior of other countries. As noted earlier, the argument that favors the special importance of certain key sectors and technologies identifies several characteristics associated with these sectors: economies of scale, economies of "learning" and know-how, imperfect competition (e.g., barriers to entry or to technology acquisitions), and the generation of subsequent benefits (externalities) for other sectors of the economy.[5]

Although the argument in favor of certain "key" industries and technologies has appealing features, it suffers from several serious weaknesses. One weakness is the lack of an objective basis for determining precisely which industries or technologies are or will be the key ones. This leads to the further difficulty of adjudicating between the competing claims advanced by both the scientific and business communities in advocating the prospective positive externalities and learning-curve benefits associated with the technologies or industries they favor. Compounding this difficulty is the rapidity of change as to what constitutes key or critical technologies, even if an initial cut at identifying them could be made objectively. For example, it seems likely that the digital technology in which Japan's advanced development of high-definition television has been concentrating will be leap-frogged by the development of fiber optics in which the U.S. has been leading. Moreover, the process of competition and adaptation may render the position of leadership in a supposedly key technology transitory and vulnerable. Thus, U.S. production of semiconductors, after several years of ceding market share to Japanese producers, has in the past two years caught up with and overtaken the Japanese market share, while enhancing the dominance of U.S. producers in the advanced microprocessor part of the industry.

SYNERGIES BETWEEN ECONOMIC AND MILITARY INSTRUMENTS

As a general proposition, the use or credible threat to use economic instruments to confer rewards or impose penalties can enhance the capacity of military instruments to influence the behavior of other countries by the use of force, or by a credible threat to use it. In some circumstances, economic instruments may substitute for military instruments. Despite these potentially important interactive relationships between economic and military instruments, too little of the discussion and analysis of economic instruments has considered

---

[5]See the discussion in Chapter Three above.

their use in conjunction with that of military instruments—to which we now turn.

The following examples suggest some opportunities for the synergistic use of economic and military instruments for defense-related purposes.

Arms Trade and Arms Control

One of the acute problems with which the post–Cold War era is likely to be afflicted is that relating to the proliferation of increasingly effective conventional weapons. The $30 billion annual weapons market is propelled by powerful economic incentives alluded to earlier, that impinge on the major weapon producers—the United States, Russia, China, France, and Britain, as well as numerous "second-tier" producers, including Brazil, Israel, North and South Korea, Argentina, and Taiwan—and the often still more powerful political-ethnic-diplomatic incentives and aspirations of the weapon buyers in the Middle East, Asia, Eastern Europe, and other potentially unstable regions of the world.

The question then arises whether the military balances in these regions might be made more secure by controlling weapon *imports* into countries of the region and by controlling weapon *exports* from the major suppliers to these regions. If a practicable answer to this question exists, it is likely to depend on the synergistic use of economic, military, and political-diplomatic instruments of policy.[6] For example, it may be possible to establish analytically the specific categories of weapons that would be most destabilizing in particular regional arms balances. For example, such weapons as advanced land and sea mines, submarines, and long-range and accurate cruise missiles might be especially destabilizing in the Middle East region. For such "high leverage" items, it may be possible to establish a "market stabilizing mechanism" that would either prohibit the ex-

---

[6]An ongoing RAND research project, under the leadership of Ken Watman and Marcy Agmon, considers the synergistic use of economic and military instruments to establish and enforce such controls in the arms trade. Kenneth Watman, Marcy Agmon, Charles Wolf, Jr., *Controlling Conventional Arms Transfers*, Santa Monica, Calif.: RAND, MR-369-USDP, 1994.

port of such systems entirely, or, in exceptional cases where the exporting country has compelling economic needs (specifically Russia, for which weapon exports represent such a large traditional source of foreign exchange earnings), to establish a compensatory fund subscribed by the five member countries and by other possible contributors to offset the opportunity costs incurred by forgone sales.

Another economic instrument that could be invoked to support the market stabilizing mechanism might be an arrangement for preemptive counterbidding by a threatened member of the region to induce the seller to refrain from the impending sale. If, for example, one of the five major sellers were seriously considering the sale of a high-leverage system, e.g., submarines, to Iran or Iraq, Saudi Arabia might be given a right of first refusal to preempt the sale.

Finally, in addition to these carrots, an enforcement stick might be invoked in the form of denying access to the commercial markets of the five member countries by any individual firm in an exporting country that violates the restrictions provided by the market-stabilizing regime.

Dual-Use Technology in Reverse

We have referred earlier to the possibility of introducing as one criterion in the selection of new military technology the possibility that the selected technology would also have commercial applications and spillover benefits. The process can also be viewed in reverse. In considering military tasks and missions, instead of developing advanced technology to enhance the performance of these missions, it may be more effective in using (and saving) military resources in general, and military R&D resources in particular, to "piggyback" on the civil sector, rather than developing *de novo* new technology for the military. Rather than developing new sensors or new software for military guidance systems, it may be more efficient for the conduct of military programs to investigate thoroughly the availability of current or impending counterpart technologies in the civil commercial sectors that might be given a marginal tilt or spin to enable them to be used effectively for the military purposes that are sought.

The Effects of Economic Growth on Defense Capabilities

One of the most striking examples of the use of economic instruments of power to complement military instruments is provided by South Korea's record in the past several years. In this instance, the relevant economic instruments have been Korea's remarkable record of economic and technological progress—average annual real growth of its gross national product of 8 percent during the past two decades, and more than doubling the real volume of its international trade in the past decade)—thereby providing leverage for Korea's efforts to establish formal diplomatic and economic relationships with Russia and China. In turn, these relationships have significantly reduced, if not permanently removed, the provision by Russia and China of military aid to North Korea. The bottom-line result is, in effect, to reduce the probability of aggression from the North, and to improve the military balance between North and South Korea in favor of the South.

Thus, South Korea's economic instruments, as reflected by its expanded economic and technological base, and the attraction to Russia and China of increased economic relations with South Korea, have contributed to a substantial enhancement of South Korea's military parity relative to that of the North.

A less benign example of the powerful effects of economic growth on defense and security capabilities is provided by China's recent record. China is the fastest growing of the major countries in the world, with an average real rate of growth 2 or 3 times that of the other major countries. With this expanding base, China is the only major country whose military capabilities and projection forces are substantially growing, while those of other countries have indeed been receding. Whether and how this expansion in China's military capabilities will be used is likely to be among the most serious security issues facing the world over the next decade.

Japan presents another instance of the overarching effects on defense capabilities and resources that result from economic growth. Over the past decade Japan's significant military modernization and enhancement has been sustained by the allocation of approximately

1 percent of the Japanese GNP to defense uses. In a period of rapid economic growth, this constant 1-percent parameter was applied to an expanding base, thereby providing substantial resources—$2 or 3 billion in constant prices—each year for use in increasing Japan's military capabilities. But the Japanese economy has experienced serious setbacks in recent years, resulting in negative growth in 1992 and the prospect of probably much lower real rates of growth during the rest of the 1990s. In these circumstances, whether the resources that are allocated to maintaining, let alone enhancing, Japanese military capabilities if the 1-percent figure is maintained, or whether that parameter will be raised, is likely to be the focus of sharp political controversy in Japan.

Chapter Six

CONCLUDING OBSERVATIONS

Several points can be inferred from the preceding discussion. First, the economic dimensions of national security are complex, interrelated, and widely ramified. In the policy arena, these complexities and ramifications result in responsibilities that are shared, overlapping, and sometimes ambiguous among government agencies.

Second, it is difficult to define precisely the meaning of "economic security," or its cognate, the "economic dimensions of national security." Still, a useful framework for this purpose is to distinguish between the national-security effects of economic policies, and the economic effects of national-security policies: The former include, for example, the rate and stability of U.S. economic growth; the latter include the potential spin-offs from dual-use technology, as well as the use of economic power for national-security ends.

Third, while the economic dimensions of national security have acquired increased interest and emphasis in the post–Cold War era, as well as the particular attention of the Clinton administration, these dimensions are generic: They pervade the meaning and interpretation of national security, whether one is referring to the Cold War or to the post–Cold War period, to the Clinton administration, or to prior or successor ones. The differences relate to the emphasis and priority accorded to these dimensions, rather than to acknowledgment of their relevance to national security.

Fourth, the roles of different agencies of government and different policy levers that are relevant for considering the economic dimensions of national security vary widely, depending on which particular dimensions one focuses on. To the extent that the focus is on na-

85

tional-security dimensions of economic policy—including the expanded meaning of "economic security," the relevance of stability and predictability in the international economic and financial environment, the putative importance of key industries and sectors, and so on—the key levers of these aspects of economic security reside in agencies other than the DoD, the National Security Council, and the intelligence community. To the extent that one focuses instead on the economic dimensions of national security policy, the relevant policy levers are ones over which the DoD has greater influence.

Fifth, for the coordinated and synergistic use of economic instruments, on the one hand, and military instruments, on the other, in effective planning and execution of economic security, joint efforts by the DoD and the agencies that are principally responsible for economic policy in the government are essential.

Finally, notwithstanding the importance of giving greater attention to economic security and its instruments in the post–Cold War era, there may be a tendency to discount prematurely and too heavily the classic military instruments whose role has been central in the "old thinking" of the prior era. The international environment of the new era will be characterized by uncertainty, unpredictability, and instability. Many and probably most of the instabilities will warrant a response of neglect—benign or otherwise—from the United States either because of limitations on our power to bring about predictable improvement and relief or on grounds of limited national interests in trying to do so. But, as events as different from one another as Desert Storm, Somalia, and Bosnia suggest, some instabilities may warrant the application of either or both military and economic instruments, by the United States acting alone or, more likely and more frequently, acting in coalition with others. Choosing how and when to respond in such circumstances will entail an enhanced capacity for resilience and flexibility in the design and deployment of both economic and military instruments.

Appendix

CONFERENCE ON THE ECONOMIC DIMENSIONS OF NATIONAL SECURITY FEBRUARY 7–8, 1992, RAND, SANTA MONICA, CA

PARTICIPANTS

Richard Danzig (Latham and Watkins)

Paul Davis (RAND)

George Donohue (RAND)

John Ferch (National Intelligence Council)

Karen Elliott House (*Wall Street Journal*)

Gary Hufbauer (Georgetown University)

Sam Huntington (Harvard University)

Michael Kennedy (RAND)

Thomas Longstreth (Joint Staff)

Michael May (Lawrence Livermore Lab)

Ruben Mettler (TRW)

C. Richard Neu (RAND)

Jonathan Pollack (RAND)

Michael Rich (RAND)

Harry Rowen (Stanford University)

Larry Seaquist (OUSDP)

Abram Shulsky (OUSDP)

Herbert Stein (American Enterprise Institute)

Jim Thomson (RAND)

Albert Wheelon

Albert Wohlstetter

Charles Wolf, Jr. (RAND)

Charles Zwick (Southeast Banking Corporation)